Political Musings

Political Musings

Turmoil in the Middle East

Sanu Kainikara

Vij Books India Pvt Ltd
New Delhi (India)

First Published in 2016

ISBN : 978-93-85563-53-9 (Hardback)

ISBN : 978-93-85563-54-6 (ebook)

Designed and Setting by

Vij Books India Pvt Ltd
2/19, Ansari Road, Darya Ganj, New Delhi - 110002 (India)
www.vijbooks.com

Dedicated to the memory of

Tara 'Lola' Menon (1949-2015)

Sister and Friend—sorely missed

Whose *Joie de Vivre* remains unmatched!

BOOKS BY THE SAME AUTHOR

Papers on Air Power

Pathways to Victory

Red Air: Politics in Russian Air Power

Australian Security in the Asian Century

A Fresh Look at Air Power Doctrine

Friends in High Places

Seven Perennial Challenges to Air Forces

The Art of Air Power: Sun Tzu Revisited

At the Critical Juncture

Essays on Air Power

The Bolt from the Blue

The Asian Crucible

The Indian History Series: From Indus to Independence

Volume I: Prehistory to the Fall of the Mauryas

Volume II: The Classical Age

Volume III: The Disintegration of Empires

Content

AUTHOR'S PREFACE

This book is a collection of essays that were written between January and December 2015, as commentaries and analysis of on-going events, with a marked focus on the Middle-East. Without doubt, the Middle-East was in the spotlight for the entire world throughout 2015, with the conflict in Syria continuing to rage and the fight against the Islamic State (IS) not abating even a little bit. The happenings in both Syria and Iraq reverberated across Europe and also some parts of Asia and it can be said with absolute certainty that there was no nation in the world that was not influenced in some way or the other by the conflict. The rushing currents of change emanating from the Middle-East touched the entire international community.

Commenting on a contemporary event can be considered the first draft of history, although it is also a fact that such 'initial' analyses may not serve any overarching purpose in some cases, especially if the analysis proves to be incorrect into the near-term future. Writing about the here and now involves a certain amount of imagination, which could be either right or wrong, and is almost completely dependent on the individual ethos of the analyst. This is the case with the essays collected in this book, the analysis and their veracity, or lack thereof, is a function purely of my own intuitions and understanding of the situation as it was developing.

A majority of the essays in the book have been published by the Eurasia Review over the year and I have received both brickbats and bouquets for my analysis from a range of people, indicating the wide interest that the progress of events in the Middle-East, and to a lesser extent South Asia, elicit. This book is the first of what I hope will be a series of collection of political essays marking the passage of each year. They would, over a period of time, form yearbooks to mark the significant events of the 12-month period while also providing an analysis as they were understood at the time. I sincerely hope that these yearbooks will gradually grow into reference material for future analysts and scholars to study the events to which I bear remote witness. As a student of international politics, nothing would delight me more.

Sanu Kainikara

Canberra

February 2016

'All men and women are to each other

The limbs of a single body, each of us drawn

From life's shimmering essence. God's perfect pearl;

And when this life we share wounds one of us,

All share the hurt as if it were our own,

You, who will not feel another's pain,

You forfeit the right to be called human.'

Poem *'Bani Adam'* in *Gulistan*,

Saadi Shirazi (1210-1292), Renowned Persian Poet

Translated by *Richard Jeffrey Newman*,

Selections from Saadi's Gulistan

'Recognising an existing regime should not be regarded as implying approval. It should be regarded merely as acknowledgement of existing facts. The West, in the end, came to admit this as regards the USSR, but it did not learn from this experience the unwisdom of tardiness in acknowledging regimes which cannot be upset without world war.'

Bertrand Russell,

Has Man A Future, published 1961, p. 119

INTRODUCTION
2015 – THE YEAR THAT WAS...

The common point of discussion throughout 2015 was the on-going and bloody Syrian Civil War and the conflict between the international coalition and the Islamic State (IS) mainly in Iraq and Syria. The Civil War does not seem have any logical conclusion and the fight against the IS, by some of the most powerful military forces in the world, does not seem to be making any visible progress. The reasons for this state of affairs are many and defies any comprehensive listing, since most of them overlap and some of them are contradictory. The conflict in the heart of the Middle-East also spawned a number of subsidiary actions that made temporary splashes in the collective conscious of the free world and died along with its ripples.

Saudi Arabia and the Yemeni Adventure

The year started with an outwardly seamless change in the leadership in Saudi Arabia, in a display of predestined, calculated and rapid transition of power from the old to the new guard, on the death of King Abdullah. For the first time in the history of the desert kingdom a grandson of Abdul-Aziz al-Saud, the founder of the al-Saud dynasty, was elevated to the ruling elite as the Deputy Crown Prince, the de facto second in line for succession. King Salman, the new king, has made a visible effort to consolidate the power of the 'Sudairi Seven', brothers born to Hasa bint Ahmed al-Sudairi, and their progeny, much to the chagrin of a large number of other royalty who feel sidelined from the core of power. However, tribal loyalty has been an indelible and critical part of the smooth transition of power in Saudi Arabia and this time has been no exception.

King Salman inherits a foreign policy that is in tatters. For the past two decades, Saudi Arabia under King Abdullah had made a series of foreign policy blunders that culminated with the kingdom's vehement opposition to the 'Arab Spring' that started in 2011. Then there was the still on-going estrangement with the US, their primary guarantor of security. The US reaction to the Arab Spring was more of an eye opener for Saudi Arabian policy makers, than was the unexpected rapidity with which the phenomenon spread across the region. This started an internal analysis within the ruling cabal regarding the future security of the nation and the reliance that could be placed on the US. The seed of doubt regarding assured US support was one of the reasons for the Saudi Arabian leadership opting for a far more proactive and forceful foreign policy throughout 2015, rather than continuing the traditional soft approach and reliance on the economic might of the kingdom.

Saudi Arabia today is surrounded by neighbours, most of whom are all in some sort of turmoil. However, it is besotted with the idea of subverting the rising influence of Iran even if it means resorting to short-sighted policies that would come back home roost. There is no doubt that King Salman inherited a foreign policy that had stalled and was in the doldrums. While it is early days yet, the question that has to be asked is whether or not the king has the will and the energy to evolve a proactive but non-Iran centric policy. At this juncture it seems that the answer is no.

Yemen has historically been the battleground where the proxy war between Iran and Saudi Arabia has always played out. In late March, Saudi Arabia led a ten-nation coalition into direct military intervention in the civil war in Yemen, by launching an air campaign, much like the US-led coalition effort to fight the IS. Yemen has been in conflict off and on for a long time based on a 14-century old schism between Sunnis and Shias. For historic reasons Saudi Arabia has never looked kindly at Yemen. The current conflict is the continuation of antagonism between the two countries that can be traced back to 1991, when Yemen, as a temporary member of the UN Security Council, voted against the US-led intervention to liberate Kuwait from Iraqi occupation. By early 2014, Yemen had become the battleground for the proxy war between Iran and Saudi Arabia. Iran supports the Houthis who had taken over Sana'a and had also captured most of the capital, Aden. The rise of the Houthis in Yemen can also be traced back to Saudi Arabia's miscalculation of their resilience and also their preoccupation with containing Al Qaeda in the Arabian Peninsula (AQAP).

The Saudi Arabia-led intervention is based on the belief that a Houthi takeover would lead to Yemen becoming a Shia-ruled satellite state of Iran, a situation that is unacceptable for Saudi Arabia. A deeper analysis however reveals that the rise of the Houthis is not the fundamental reason for the sectarian polarisation in Yemen, but a reaction to sectarianism. The current conflict is a sparring proxy war between Iran and Saudi Arabia for regional hegemony. Confrontation between Yemen and Saudi Arabia, whether supported externally or not, has never been far from the surface and Saudi Arabia has always been unwilling to live with a rebellious and inimical neighbour strategically placed at the kingdom's soft underbelly.

By end-April, the Sunni-Shia fault line that was already etched in the region became clearly visible on the sands of the Middle-East. Almost all the nations of the region were involved in some sort of conflict, brought about primarily by the Iran-Saudi Arabia rivalry for political and religious domination of the region. The conflict in Yemen is an endemic indicator of interventions to shore up conflicting national interests that benefit nobody, and achieve only fleeting moments of vaingloriousness for some of the participating nations. It is also noteworthy that Saudi Arabia initiated a move to create the embryonic infrastructure of an 'Arab Army' but so far this does not seem to have achieved much traction with the other Arab nations.

The direct intervention by Saudi Arabia and its Arab allies in Yemen is indicative of the new leadership's determination to assert their power in a demonstrable manner. It also shows the Saudi Arabian foreign policy being decidedly moved away from the discrete form that had been practised for so many decades. However, like all military interventions across the world, this one has already become messy and protracted. The poverty of Yemen does not provide any assurance of the campaign being short and swift. There will be no immediate end to the conflict in Yemen, the only assurance is that the already poor people of Yemen will continue to suffer into the future, while external elements fight to determine their future.

By June, the conflict in Yemen had ground down to an almost stalemate condition, it was unclear whether anyone was winning and if so who. It seemed to a neutral observer that the only beneficiary of the intervention was AQAP who had managed to form alliances with some factions in the conflict and who were no longer being targeted by the Saudi Arabian coalition. This situation defied logic, since AQAP is sworn to derail the al Saud rule of Saudi Arabia. Further, if the Saudi Arabians had hoped to provoke Iran into more direct involvement in the civil war, they failed. Iran maintained a studied and constant position, continuing its covert support for the Houthis but not allowing themselves to be incited into precipitate action. The only losers at the moment are the common people of Yemen.

South Asia –Muddling Along

Also in June, Bangladesh came into the limelight, for all the wrong reasons—there was a spate of daylight murders of liberal 'bloggers' by religious fanatics and a deathly silence from the broader society and inaction from the government. There has been an on-going no-holds-barred fight between the two major political parties—the Awami League and the Bangladesh National Party—for some time for control of the nation. However, in more recent times this fight has become part of the sectarian violence and rapidly spreading religious fundamentalism that has swept into the streets of Bangladesh. This is a classic case of politically supported fundamentalist agitation going out of control and taking on a life of its own.

Bangladesh is reeling under a creeping culture of religious fundamentalism and intolerance perpetuated by groups who claim to be 'protecting' the Islamic religion. Perhaps nothing could be farther from the truth. The government's inability, or reluctance, to curtail these atrocities and the soft approach that it adopted to violence perpetuated on religious grounds did nothing the improve the situation or its credibility. Both India and Pakistan played to their own agendas in the confusion, although they did not yet reach the level of proxy confrontations. In the meantime, the space for basic individual freedoms—of expression, religion and the expectation of the rule of law—was shrinking fast in Bangladesh. The time to act has perhaps already come and gone.

At the same time Pakistan was also beset with internal problems stemming from religious fundamentalism and related terrorism. The country has used terrorism as a tool of foreign policy for long, although it is officially denied. The current challenges are proof that self-serving strategies invariably come home to roost faster than thought to be possible, especially when the state machinery is inept and the borders porous. The military continues to run the country, even though a nominal democratically elected government is in place. There is belief in some quarters that the ISI has gradually evolved into the military's own Frankenstein, an entity beholden to nobody. However, analysis of recent events show this belief to be incorrect, the ISI is firmly controlled by the Chief of the Army Staff and bends to his bidding.

Baluchistan meanwhile continued to fester with state-sponsored proxies perpetuating violent action against Baluchi liberation groups. The story of failed policies on Baluchistan persisted unabated through the year in review. The Army in the meantime carried on with its much advertised campaign against insurgents and terrorist groups in North Waziristan, although it has become apparent that the action is selective and unlikely to bring about any holistic dividends to the broader security environment. The operations now seem to be focused on getting rid of groups that are inimical to the Army's agenda. It is obvious, as always, that the Pakistani military continues to function within a world of their own, oblivious to any other input and with no indication that there is cognisance and acknowledgement of the democratically elected government and its policies. In such a scenario it is not surprising that IS has made substantial inroads into the existing fundamentalist religious groups that operate without any check in the country. The Pakistani regime has adopted a denial program for all the ills that it lets lose in the region, converting double-standards and policy backflips into an art form.

Turkey – On a Tangential Trajectory

For nearly four years as the Syrian Civil War raged, Turkey had been sitting on their hands as a spectator, even attempting to strategically distance itself from the Western coalition fighting the IS and NATO, of which it is full-fledged member. Even when the town of Kobani, on the border between Syria and Turkey, was being ravaged and destroyed, Turkish armoured units sat a mere two kilometres away without taking any action. In August, as a result of a terrorist attack within the country, Turkey reluctantly joined the fight against the IS. Thereafter it has tried to move closer to NATO and permitted the use of its airbases by the coalition for mounting missions in Iraq and Syria and even taken part in some token strikes. Even so, Turkey continues to maintain a defused strategy towards the IS.

Turkey has been ruled by the AKP for more than a decade now and their foreign policy has completely failed in the wake of the Syrian Civil War followed by the rise of the IS. There are three underlying factors that shape Turkey's foreign policy—the Islamic agenda of the ruling AKP, which denies the legitimacy of Tukey's secularism as a historic travesty; the absolute determination that Bashar al-Assad must step down in Syria; and containing and neutralising any Kurdish attempt at gaining even the slightest modicum of autonomy. AKP's inability to garner a majority in the 7 June elections can be attributed to peoples' reaction to the vaulting ambition of its leader President Recep Tayyip Erdogan, the overt Islamisation that was embarked upon, and the fact that the party was seen to be too close to the perpetrators of the Arab Spring, mainly the Muslim Brotherhood. Political Islam has always sat very lightly in Turkey.

However, the terrorist attacks and the subsequent security fears gave the AKP a majority in the run-off elections held in November. Even after joining the fight, Tukey has been consciously targeting the Kurdish militia in order to ensure that they do not have an opportunity to demand autonomy. It is the urgency of keeping the Kurds under check that makes Turkey demand the creation of a 'Buffer Zone' at its southern borders with Syria. Only such a zone can ensure that Turkish Kurds do not establish a geographic link with the more successful Syrian Kurdish militia. In fact the Syrian Kurds are the only ones to have had any success in fighting the IS throughout the year. In a bid to delegitimise the Kurdish movement, Turkey has conveniently equated the IS and the Kurdish militia, the PKK. By continuing to follow a confused foreign policy, Erdogan has pushed Turkey into a one-way street with very little manoeuvring room and almost no friends to bail them out. An interesting situation for a nation that was even two years ago considered the epitome of Islamic democracy.

Syria and the Islamic State

By around August it was clear to all observers that Bashar al-Assad's control over Syria was limited to few geographic pockets and that his government's ability to take the fight to the IS was in terminal decline. The Civil War had by then been fought continuously for four years and there was no end in sight. It was also equally clear that the IS was making headway in their conquest, while both Saudi

Arabia and Turkey continued to play truants, supporting disparate Islamic groups and pursuing their own narrowly focused agenda. In fact the entire US-led coalition seemed to be in disarray. The Kurds—spread across Turkey, Syria, Iraq and Iran—became a force to reckon with, much to Turkey's chagrin. The Iraqi Kurds had already carved out a de facto autonomous zone and the Syrian Kurds were gaining in strength. Reading between the lines, this could well have been President Erdogan's real reason for joining the fight—to stop the Turkish Kurds from gaining any leverage with the international community. At this stage there was no prospect of peace in sight.

In analysing the IS and its continuing strength it can be seen that the creation of the entity was not a revolutionary process, but one of evolution—a culmination of years of encroaching religious fundamentalism and fanaticism, fanned by the ever-present Sunni-Shia divide. The catalyst in this process was the ill-conceived rule by the Maliki government that alienated the Iraqi Sunnis leading to unmitigated anarchy in the country. The remarkable staying power that IS has demonstrated in the face of concerted attacks by some of the most powerful air forces in the world indicates that it has a coherent strategy in place to stake its claim as a 'state', even though such a situation is highly unpalatable to the West.

Throughout 2015, IS displayed all the trappings of a sovereign state—holding territory that it governed, however despicable that rule may have been, and providing civic services to the regions under their control. This is why the belief that both Turkey and Saudi Arabia harbour, that the IS is a 'controllable' entity, is tantamount to living in a fools' paradise. The fundamental objective of the IS is to recreate the ancient Ottoman Empire, which would necessitate swallowing both Turkey and Saudi Arabia. Towards this end the IS has mounted a systemic attack on the concept of the legality of geographical borders, the sovereignty nation-states, and the idea of religion and the executive as being mutually independent, as Western concepts, to be shunned. Such radical ideas can only be countered by other equally prescient ideas, not military might as the current endeavour seems to be focused on.

Nationalism is an alien concept in the framework of the Middle-East, where tribal loyalties transcend all other attachments and man-made geographic borders have very little meaning. The IS very cleverly exploits this 'weakness' and garners support through emphasising religious and sectarian groupings. It is relatively easier for the people to accept this idea of a geographically amorphous but religiously cohesive entity. Countering such an idea needs a clear, credible and powerful narrative—half-baked air campaigns are not going to produce any tangible result. The challenge is to beat the morphing ideology of the IS with ideas and concepts that have better appeal than the puritanical and repressive code that is being preached. Currently the Western coalition is at a standstill mired in a fight with a paucity of ideas.

Russia – The Unpredictable Power

In mid-September, when the Assad regime seemed on the verge of collapse through sheer exhaustion, Russia entered the conflict to shore up the regime. In one fell swoop, the Russian intervention altered the geo-strategic environment in the whole of the Middle-East, making a complex situation even more complicated. Primarily the Russians upset the calculations of Turkey, which had counted on the post-Assad Syria being a Turkish vassal state.

Russia had many valid reasons to intervene in the Syrian Civil War. First, it wanted to protect its strategic interests in terms of ensuring that the only Mediterranean port available to its navy was not lost. Second, Syria had been an old ally, dating back to the immediate aftermath of World War II, the beginning of the Cold War, and now was not the time to let the country and Assad down. It also made a show of displaying the steadfastness of Russian friendship as opposed to the fluidity of US alliances as displayed when the erstwhile

Egyptian President Hosni Mubarak was under siege in the onslaught of the Arab Spring. Third, Russia wants to nip in the bud any influence that the IS can peddle abroad to its own religious fundamentalists. Fourth, Russia wants to have a decisive say in the future of the Middle-East and Syria was its stronghold to ensure this. The list of reasons is fairly long and can go on. By this intervention, Russia has emerged as a power to reckon with, a status so far denied it by the conceited West.

Russia supports a negotiated settlement to the Syrian Civil War in which Bashar al-Assad will play an important role in the transitional government. This is directly opposed to both the Turkish and Saudi Arabian viewpoints, which are single-mindedly focused on removing Assad from power as the prerequisite for any negotiated settlement to the conflict. Russia stands firmly with Syria and is aligned with Iran in considering the final outcome.

An unexpected fallout of the Russian intervention was that it exposed the complete failure of the US-led Western strategy to contain the Syrian Civil War and to defeat the IS. It was almost immediately apparent that the one-year old campaign was not progressing as it was meant to in the original plans. Russia was therefore able to shape the environment to suit its own preferred options. It wants to counter the US influence in the region, a bigger stake in the broader Middle-Eastern political game play, and to create an enhanced sphere of influence on its periphery. When Turkey thought that the Russian influence was increasing it initiated an ill-advised step of shooting down a Russian fighter aircraft, hoping that the reactions would make a confrontation between US and NATO on the one side and Russia on the other inevitable. However, Russia is engaged in a long term game of patience, perseverance and persistence and did not succumb to the temptation. It demonstrated a remarkably mature attitude, which made Turkey's NATO allies move back a step from it, obviously not the reaction that Erdogan had hoped to elicit.

And so the Middle-East muddled through 2015, the only constant being the misery of the Iraqi and Syrian people.

1

THE KING IS DEAD-LONG LIVE THE KING
SAUDI ARABIA: A LEGACY OF FOREIGN POLICY BLUNDERS

Much is being written about the 'peaceful' transition of power and the rapid administrative overhaul that has been undertaken by King Salman in the fortnight or so that he has been in power in Saudi Arabia. The Saudi newspapers are trumpeting the changes as heralding a new era within the kingdom. Nothing could be farther from the truth.

Saudi Arabia is geographically surrounded by disorder ever since the beginning of the Arab Spring in 2011—Syria in the west; Iraq in the north; Bahrain in the east; and Yemen in the south. The threat perception of the kingdom is therefore magnified, considering the regional and the increasingly chaotic domestic factors. At the death of King Abdullah, Salman bin Abdulaziz Al-Saud (79) his half-brother who had been the Crown Prince for the past two and a half years, assumed the throne seamlessly. At the same time the then Deputy Crown Prince appointed by King Abdullah, Muqrin bin Abdulaziz Al-Saud (69), was elevated to the position of Crown Prince. Prince Muqrin is yet another half-brother of both King Abdullah and King Salman. Unlike other traditional monarchies, the Saudi monarchy has practised succession from brother to brother, rather than as an entrenched patriarchy. So this succession was not in any way extraordinary.

A smooth succession in Saudi Arabia is important because of the kingdom's criticality to regional stability and also its position as the major global energy supplier. It holds centre stage in Middle-Eastern politics and in the international religious debate centred on Islam. At least for now, stability of Saudi Arabia is an essential criterion for global stability. Now that at least temporary stability has been achieved, the new administration will have to address growing challenges to the well-being of the kingdom. At the outset, King Salman reiterated his commitment to the continuance of policies forged by the previous king, which had a calming influence on the region, especially the Gulf nations, Egypt, and in an indirect manner Turkey. However, he was also quick to replace the old guard, especially the influential and powerful adviser to King Abdullah, Khaled al-Tuwaijri— who is now being blamed for the flawed foreign policy decisions of the old regime—by his own son, Mohammad bin Salman Al-Saud (34), who was appointed the Minister of Defence (Defense) and also the head of the Royal Court, replacing al-Tuwaijri as the king's adviser. At the same time, for the first time a grandson of Abdulaziz, Muhammad bin Nayef bin Abdulaziz Al-Saud (55), was appointed the Deputy Crown Prince.

The Importance of these Appointments

Abdulaziz Al-Saud, the founder of the dynasty had many wives and therefore, most of his sons are only half-brothers to each other. In such a scenario, matrilineal identity assumes greater importance in terms of loyalty and closeness between brothers. An alliance of seven full brothers, called the Sudairi Seven born to Abdulaziz and Hassa bint Ahmed al-Sudairi, considered to have been his favourite wife, form a powerful clique within the Royal family. (The Sudairi Seven are Fahd, Sultan, Abdulrahman, Nayef, Turki, Salman, and Ahmed.) Their influence spans the entire officialdom from top to bottom and is pervasively visible across the entire kingdom. The appointment of Muhammad bin Nayef has to be seen within this perspective—since he will invariably be the king after next (or the next king if Crown Prince Muqrin predeceases King Salman) he will perpetuate the rule of the Sudairi Seven's rule and lineage. Needless to say this will marginalise hundreds of princes some of whom are themselves sons of kings. There can be no assurance that dissent within the Royal family will not spill out into the public arena when the first grandson of the founder assumes office, sometime in the near future.

However, these two appointments from within the Sudairi Seven fold was necessary for consolidating power in the immediate post-succession period. These moves are based on the concept of 'asabiya' an unwritten code of tribal solidarity, especially in testing times. Perhaps this code will be the glue that holds the kingdom together in the days to come, which are bound to be turbulent in a number of ways.

King Abdullah's Legacy—A Tarnished Foreign Policy

King Abdullah started his official rule in 2005, although he had been the de-facto ruler since 1995 when his half-brother King Fahd was incapacitated, with conciliatory gestures towards women and the Shia minority. By reaching out to these two completely disenfranchised groups, Abdullah initiated an 'inclusive' forward movement for the kingdom. He created the first co-educational University in the kingdom and gradually brought Saudi Arabia into the WTO, initiatives seen both domestically and internationally as the first steps of a progressive monarch. However, the events of 11 September 2001 put these initiatives into the shadow since the king had to use his considerable diplomatic influence to safeguard the kingdom from becoming a hotbed of terrorism. Almost at the same time, arch rivals Iran had started to rise as an alternative power centre in the region. The direct threats to Saudi Arabia overshadowed the king's well-intentioned domestic reform agenda.

King Abdullah was less than impressed by the US for the hands-off approach that it displayed during the initial development of the Arab Spring, and the subsequent support for the anti-Mubarak protesters in Egypt. He decided to follow a more independent foreign policy for the kingdom and also voiced the beginning of a distrust of US intentions in the region. However, the kingdom's foray into regional, and in an indirect manner, international politics as an independent entity was not the success that Abdullah expected it to be. A detailed look at the foundations of Saudi Arabia's foreign policy and the on-going initiatives clearly indicate the failures and the morass that the nation has moved into of its own volition.

Foreign Policy Blunders

From the 1970s, when the impoverished kingdom stepped out as an oil-rich nation bent on becoming the sinecure of the world, Saudi Arabia has followed a foreign policy of pursuing global Islamic solidarity in order to ensure its own political and economic stability. Its overflowing richness permitted it to take the lead in this endeavour, primarily through buying off opposition. However, even after more than 40 years, Saudi Arabia and its ruling dynasty has not been able to win people's hearts and minds, either domestically, regionally or internationally. Even after ruling the kingdom for 19 years, King Abdullah was not able to achieve any consensus with the other regional nations regarding the way forward to ensure common stability and security.

Saudi Arabia, aspiring to and claiming the leadership of the region, took only hesitant and small steps to ensure stability as the region erupted in turmoil and chaos in early 2011. Thereafter the Saudi foreign policy initiatives make up a long list of self-serving actions that could be loosely clubbed together as 'blunders' and, which collectively diminish the already tarnished image of the kingdom.

Egypt

The worst case was the role that Saudi Arabia played in Egypt, especially in the coup against Muhammad Morsi who was leading a democratically elected Muslim Brotherhood government. Saudi Arabia supported the military administrator (dictator) turned 'elected' President Abdel Fattah al-Sisi, in ousting the Morsi government and continues to prop him up with enormous financial donations. During this upheaval the Saudi monarchy willingly accepted the death of thousands of Egyptian pro-democracy protesters in order to ensure that the democratic movement did not spread to the kingdom. The acceptance of these deaths was appalling, and the fact remains that Saudi Arabia sacrificed Egypt's fledgling democracy at the altar of the monarchy's self-interest. From this point of view, the al-Sisi government cannot be allowed to fail under any circumstances and therefore Saudi Arabia provides unconditional support to the regime. In the long-term, this support itself could become a self-defeating double edged sword.

Bahrain

The next Saudi foreign policy initiative was the vicious suppression of pro-democracy protesters in Bahrain in February 2011. The movement that had taken hold in Bahrain was part of the then-spreading Arab Spring, and Saudi Arabia felt that it could not allow it to burgeon into anything of consequence. Even though the Saudi intervention was, at least outwardly, at the request of the ruler of Bahrain, it cannot be viewed as anything other than an opportunistic invasion of the country by Saudi Arabia and the UAE. With direct Saudi assistance Bahrain continues to suppress, forcefully, pro-freedom demonstrators—but the world has moved on and there is not even any mention of the on-going repression in any world forum. While the intervention may have achieved its desired objective of perpetuating, at least for the time being, the rule of a Sunni ruler over a majority Shia population, it did not win any friends for Saudi Arabia and its autocratic king.

Syria

From the beginning Saudi Arabia supported the hard line Salafi factions against President Assad, purely because he belongs to an obscure Shia sect and is supported by Iran. The Saudis also thought it necessary to play a hands-on role in the rebellion in Syria to counter the moves by Turkey and Qatar, both of whom were interested in assuming a more direct role to ensure the entrenchment of their influence after the Assad regime was removed by the rebels. Saudi Arabia's ambition to be the leader of the Sunni world would not let the King take a more conciliatory role even with his so-called Sunni allies. This in-fighting between their external supporters confused the anti-Assad forces and gave birth to a group that has now morphed into the Islamic State (IS). Of course it must not be forgotten that the embryo of the IS was hatched during the US-led operations in Iraq.

From a humanitarian perspective the Syrian Civil War has created over nine million refugees, the largest the world has yet seen belonging to one single country. The IS is currently being held in check only by the air strikes being carried out by the US-led coalition. While Saudi Arabia is a part of this coalition, it has restricted its operations to Iraqi territory and is still trying to bracket the removal of President Assad with the fight against the IS. Their overarching consideration is to diminish Iranian influence and to place a Saudi-friendly government in Syria. Considering that Saudi Arabia is facing its greatest direct threat in the form of a vicious organisation that proclaims their belief in the same ideals that Saudi Arabia has supported for decades, this attitude beggars belief. Truly, in this case, the vagrant cow has wandered home.

Iraq

In the decade since Saddam Hussein was overthrown by the US invasion in 2003, Iraq's strategic outlook has not changed much. It is still suffering from internal sectarian violence and with the IS threat emerging in a forceful manner in the second half of 2014, the chances of an all-out Civil War erupting has become very high. Here again the sectarian bias of the Saudi monarchy was, and continues to be, highly visible. After the ouster of the Saddam regime, Nouri al-Maliki who became Prime Minister, had promised to form an inclusive government. However, he turned out to be even more biased and sectarian than the Saudis. Much to the chagrin of King Abdullah, the Sunnis in Iraq were sidelined and the Saudi king felt compelled to create and nurture an insurgency in order to undermine the political process and broader stability of Iraq. This was the kernel from which the ISIS and subsequently the IS grew. Conciliation and dialogue has not formed the language of Saudi diplomacy. Their policy towards Iraq from 1990 has been negative and one that can truly be described as being crafted without looking beyond immediate gains. Instead of creating—through applying their considerable influence within Iraq and with their US allies—a consensus government, the Saudi diplomatic establishment was pursuing their overriding objective of subverting the growing Iranian influence. Short sightedness made immediate gains look strategic achievements and the ruling elite seems to have been dazzled by their own 'brilliance'. Iraq now is in the throes of an existentialist threat and if it is overrun by the IS, everyone knows the next target.

Saudi Arabia had severed diplomatic relations with Iraq in 1990 when Saddam Hussain invaded Kuwait. Only now under the direct threat of the IS have they belatedly initiated dialogue with the Iraqi government. By the same reasoning it would have been logical to re-establish diplomatic relations with Iraq in 2003 after Saddam Hussein was overthrown and attempts made to improve bilateral relations. Such a statesmanlike action would perhaps have paid a dividend in terms of direct influence on the fledgling democratic government. It is also conceivable that such an action would have achieved the very same end that the Saudis seek—curtailing the influence of Iran in the region. Perhaps such a nuanced understanding of strategic diplomacy was beyond the conceptual capability of Saudi foreign policy experts. The use of terrorist groups as strategic tools of national foreign policy, as was attempted, was never going to work in the long term.

What is palpable in Saudi actions in Iraq, and very broadly in the region, is the inherent fear of a change in the regional balance of power in favour of Iran. Whether these actions are detrimental to other Arab States or could boomerang indirectly on Saudi Arabia itself seems to be a factor that is not considered in the creation of foreign policy.

Yemen

Yemen has been the traditional battlefield between Saudi Arabia and Iran. Saudi Arabia had carried out a number of stabilisation activities in Yemen over a period of time. In the past few years, all these have unravelled, commencing with the Saudi-facilitated easing out of President Saleh. The current situation wherein the Houthis—a tribe owing allegiance to, and openly supported by, Iran—have taken control of the capital and ousted the Saudi-US backed replacement 'president' is the outcome of decades of flawed Saudi Arabian policy towards Yemen. Yemen now has become a weak and fragmented State with a restive and poor tribal population that share a long and porous border with Saudi Arabia. The threat of insurgency into the kingdom is real and imminent; and at least for now Saudi Arabia does not have even the slightest clue regarding the next step to be initiated in Yemen to contain the challenge.

Afghanistan

Afghanistan has been at war for nearly three decades—against different opponents—and Saudi Arabia has been involved in some way or the other for the majority of it. The involvement started with the financial and materiel backing to the mujahedeen against the Soviet occupation, and then as moral, religious and financial support for the Taliban while they ruled Afghanistan for a short period of time. Saudi Arabia had an inordinately high level of influence on both the Taliban and their immediate puppeteers in Pakistan. However, after the US-led invasion of Afghanistan and the installation of the Karzai regime in Kabul, the Saudi foreign policy pundits opted not to use their considerable influence on Pakistan and the Taliban to force them to enter conciliatory peace talks with the Government. If the influence was used in a nuanced manner, the story of Afghanistan would have been different today. Conciliation is a concept far removed from Saudi thinking, as long as the consequences are borne by 'other' far away nations.

Even in Palestine Saudi Arabia has followed a policy of keeping the PLO and Hamas divided rather than using their influence and financial clout to effect reconciliation that would in turn bring in stability. In Libya, the Saudis backed the jihadi rebels who ousted Muammar Gaddafi and created the on-going civil war, completely destroying a once-prosperous country. That Libya was also ruled by an autocratic dictator, perhaps more liberal and certainly more secular than the Saudi monarchy, is a moot point lost in the foreign policy quagmire of Saudi Arabia.

The Fundamentals of Saudi Arabian Foreign Policy

A nation's foreign policy is a mirror of the self-perceived identity, social attitudes, and sovereign aspirations of a people. Saudi Arabia's is no exception.

The overarching identity of Saudi Arabia is its steadfast adherence to the Wahabi sect of Islam. Otherwise it is a family enterprise of the Al-Sauds, which holds together disparate regions and groups through a combination of theology and direct welfare hand-outs. The foundations of the Al-Saud rule are: pandering to intolerant clerics; a clannish centralisation of power; and continuing welfare hand-outs to the population in a mistaken and short-sighted attempt to paper over simmering dissent. From this edifice emerges a foreign policy that aims to perpetuate a sectarian and divisive version of Islam. From this it is easy to see the reason why Saudi Arabia has played a foundational role in enabling Salafist violence across the region and further afield for decades.

The run-of-the-mill Saudi citizen dislikes chaos and disorder, a trait perhaps stemming from generations of being tied to the comfort of a patriarchal family set-up that in turn is affiliated to the leadership of a tribal sheikh that goes ultimately all the way to the king. For generations the people have been 'guided' and told what to do, making one believe that they are averse to take responsibility for themselves, for the welfare of the country, or the security of the State. The common expectation is that the government will provide the wherewithal for them to meet all their needs. Individual initiative and ambition are nowhere to be seen in these conditions.

The aspirations of the people, dormant as they might be, is one aspect that the ruling family has not considered seriously since Abdulaziz Al- Saud created the kingdom in late 1932. Therefore, the primary foundation of Saudi foreign policy has always been, and continues to remain, regime or dynastic survival of the house of Saud, in other words, the sustainment of the monarchy at all costs. The other two pillars of Saudi foreign policy has been—one, to ensure that political Islam that advocates democracy is kept away from the kingdom and opposed in other countries; and two, to contain the spread of Iranian influence in the region. To this has recently been added the fundamental need to contain, defeat and eradicate the IS only because it claims to be the 'true' representatives of Salafist jihadism.

Traditionally Saudi foreign policy has been based on a soft approach—essentially using the economic might of the kingdom to exploit the influence bought through large financial incentives. This was how the Soviet occupation of Afghanistan was subverted, how Sunni militias were created in Iraq, and how a host of other activities in support of achieving their objectives have been conducted. Since regime survival is at the baseline of all foreign policy initiatives, the monarchy tends to equate domestic risks with external threats. Therefore, foreign policy becomes yet another tool to ensure that no threat to the dynasty becomes uncontrollable. The dealings with Egypt and the vehement support to the vicious suppression of the Muslim Brotherhood has to be viewed in this light. Democratic political Islam is anathema to the house of Saud.

The events of the Arab Spring and the US reaction to it, especially in Egypt, was an eye opener for King Abdullah. The US unwillingness to support President Mubarak, its long-term ally, was seen as a demonstration of the untrustworthy nature of US friendship and it shook the foundations of Saudi monarchy. In the aftermath of that episode, although another 'elected' autocrat is in place in Cairo, alarm bells are still ringing in Riyadh. The deep seated sense of vulnerability of the dynasty came to the fore and the soft approach to foreign policy was swapped for more aggressive diplomatic initiatives backed by the flexing of military muscle and even direct intervention, as in the case with Bahrain. This is almost a complete turnaround from the traditional stance of the kingdom and the rulers who never wanted to get their hands dirty.

There is a rapid reordering of the priorities of the kingdom, all the more visible with the assumption of power by King Salman. It is clear that Saudi Arabia now wants to hedge its bets with regard to a security partner. The attempt to create an authoritative axis by calling for greater unity amongst the six Gulf Cooperation Countries is an attempt to discourage popular pressure for reform stemming from the failed Arab Spring. However, years of duplicity in foreign relations and implementation of self-centred policies are coming back to haunt the house of Saud. Saudi Arabia has frittered away its influence and diplomatic weight and now does not have the independent ability to tip the balance in the region away from Iran. It was always the US that tipped the balance in favour of the Saudis, but the US reluctance to antagonise the Shia faction in the Middle-East and the acceptance of the critical role that Iran will play into the future in the region has unnerved Saudi Arabia. In a replay of its own selfishness, even the so-called friends of Saudi Arabia have started to hedge their bets.

Saudi Arabia is left with no alternative but to shore up its frayed relationship with the US. It is also clear that the kingdom needs to alter its political agenda backed by appropriate tweaking of the foreign policy. The age old policies of support to terrorist groups outside the kingdom, and muddying the waters through stoking sectarian violence to deepen the Sunni-Shia divide will not work anymore. Further, the dichotomy of support to terrorism while maintaining 'cordial' relations with Western democracies is also unravelling. The current Saudi foreign policy is a failed enterprise and has become an anachronism. Change is inevitable, if survival is to be assured.

The Islamic State – Changing Winds

The Islamic State that is now the primary threat to almost all nations in the Middle-East is the new variable in the regional and international security equation—and Saudi Arabia is the one that is most affected. Although the desert kingdom must assume at least half the responsibility for its birth, IS has conclusively changed the Saudi attitude to security and is forcing it to alter its foreign policy. First, IS is now a critical threat to the ruling monarchy and both the parties know that the socio-religious structure that exists in Saudi Arabia is fertile ground for the spread of the IS doctrine. The threat is so dire that Saudi Arabia now wants to join hands with Iraq to defeat this existentialist threat. However, there is no predictability regarding the Saudi-Iraq relationship after, and if and when, the IS is defeated, whether it will endure or return to the inherent sectarian divide. The Saudis are realising rather late that if you keep a viper for a pet, sooner or later it will bite the hand that feeds it.

Till the rise of the IS, Saudi support to terrorism in the developing world— both overt and covert—and the proselytization of the fundamentalist strain of Wahabi Islam in these countries were ignored by the Western nations. The particularly vicious actions of the IS and the sporadic but ruthless jihadi actions in the West have made these nations alter their attitude towards all terrorist/ extremist groups. It is now appreciated that support for such groups cannot be geographically compartmentalised for convenience. The Saudi government has now being coerced to join the international coalition currently fighting the IS. The Saudi rulers recognise that any display of reluctance to do so will be counterproductive to their regional leadership ambitions. Foreign policy requirements have, for the time being at least, trumped the inherent tendency in the Saudi ruling elite to create religion-tinted mayhem in vulnerable and relatively poor nations around the world as a diversion.

The IS has now emerged as a critical factor in the on-going power play in the Middle-East and therefore a deciding input in the foreign policy considerations of all nations. For Saudi Arabia, the rise of Iranian influence commensurate to the increasing power of the IS, is an untenable development.

Over the past few months, Iran has emerged as a pivotal player in the anti-IS initiatives, which has changed the course of the US-Iran dialogue. The potential of a US-Iran nuclear agreement hits at the foundation of Saudi foreign policy—the overarching need to undermine Iran.

Whatever else the IS may have achieved, there is no doubt that it has irrevocably and rapidly changed the political balance in the Middle-East. Saudi Arabia is powerless to control or manipulate this change to its advantage, a clear indication of the limit of its influence. Further, the primary objective of the US is to defeat the IS and that of the Saudis to continually deny any avenue for the spread of Iranian influence. The two are not compatible because no coalition can hope to defeat the IS without the cooperation and active participation of Iran. If anyone is aware of the direction this situation is taking, it is the Saudi monarchy. It is within the fissures in Islam that Saudi Arabia has happily played around till now—but the quagmire in Syria and the virulence of the IS have poisoned their playing field.

Challenges for the New King

The foreign policy that King Salman inherits is a legacy of failed initiatives and ill-conceived solutions to extremely complex challenges. The kingdom faces four fundamental challenges to its stability—the Islamic State, the expansion of Iranian influence in the region, a volatile oil policy, and the need for domestic reform. The IS and the implications of the coalition operations against it has been already explained.

At least for the time being, it seems that Saudi Arabia has no counter moves against Iran, especially in Yemen after the Houthi coup. With the oil prices having plummeted in the past few months, the kingdom is facing a fiscal deficit for the first time since 2011. The oil 'pundits' are of the opinion that Saudi Arabia may not be able to sustain its economy if the prices continue to tumble and therefore a cut in their production is likely sooner rather than later. King Salman has announced that he will not change the oil policy of his brother the late-King Abdullah, but there is no guarantee that it is a long-term commitment.

The demand for domestic reform is increasing in its vociferousness in Saudi Arabia, and it could not have come at a more importune time. There was no better demonstration of the double standards that the kingdom practises than the sight of its official representative marching hand-in-hand with other world leaders in the streets of Paris in a show of solidarity to protect the freedom of speech after the terrorist attack there, while at the same time flogging a person charged with posting a blog asking for domestic freedom of speech in Saudi Arabia. There is increasing tension in the kingdom with continuing demands for more individual freedoms being demanded.

The solutions to these challenges can only be achieved with a complete reprisal of both foreign and domestic policies. However, King Salman is 79 years old and unconfirmed reports indicate that he has some health issues. Saudi Arabia is now at a critical point in its history and needs dedicated and visionary leadership. The vibrant leadership that is required to steer the nation through these turbulent times is unlikely to emanate from the current leadership. The policies are bound to be more of the same!

Conclusion

The foreign policy that Saudi Arabia has so far assiduously followed has been unravelled in slow motion and is now visible as an irretrievable wreck. The blow-back from counter-productive political manipulations and reckless support for the spread of Wahabi fundamentalist Islam—as long as the violence was kept far away from the kingdom—is now raising the winds in the deserts of Saudi Arabia. The ruling dynasty, at least for the present, seems to have absolutely no clue how to face this challenge.

Instinctively Saudi Arabia is still waging proxy wars to crush democratic political Islam and continuing to use the Sunni-Shia sectarian divide to ensure that the kingdom has regional relevance and the stature to strut the Muslim world as its leader. In effect even today, all Islamist roads lead to Riyadh. It seems to be lost on the Saudi rulers that a strong nation should attempt to make their smaller allies strong for peace and stability to descend on the region. Undermining everyone else will only finally bring the very same chaos to one's own borders. In their blinkered focus on thwarting the political rise of Iran, the Saudi monarchy is missing the fact that Iran is emerging as an alternative centre of power in the region, a counter-point to Saudi Arabian hegemony. Iran is moving forward as a stable and sensible nation not afraid of democracy.

Saudi Arabia is entering uncharted waters and minefields lie ahead. It will take more than royal handouts and token words to face and overcome domestic and international challenges that at the moment look insurmountable.

King Salman and the new administration have their work cut out for them—their failure will sink the ship of the house of Al Saud, rather rapidly.

Published on 11 February 2015 in **sanukay.wordpress.com**

2

THE WAR IN YEMEN
ANOTHER POWDER KEG BLOWS UP

A ten-nation coalition led by Saudi Arabia that also comprises members of the Gulf Cooperation Council launched airstrikes in Yemen on 25th March. The Saudi ambassador to the United States stated that the operation was aimed at preventing the radical Houthi movement from taking over Yemen. The airstrikes were conducted in response to a plea for help from Yemen's President Abd Rabbuh Mansur Hadi who was removed to a safe location when his southern stronghold, the port city of Aden, was surrounded by Houthi forces. These events come in the wake of the Houthi movement's Ansar Allah fighters taking over the international airport in Aden.

The Religious Divide

Yemen is the latest in a long list of conflicts in the Middle-East that have been on-going in the past few decades. These conflicts can all be considered the modern manifestations of a 14-century old schism, based on the religious differences between Sunni and Shia Muslims, which has continually torn the region apart. These religious differences originated after the death of the Prophet Muhammad when the Sunnis believed that the next leader of Islam should be elected from a group considered to be capable of doing the job, whereas the Shias do not recognise the elected leaders and believe that the leadership should have passed to the Prophet's cousin and son-in-law Ali ibn Abu Talib, the first in a line of Imams believed to be appointed by God himself, through his Prophet Muhammad. For good measure, both Christians and Jews have joined in the fight sporadically. Islam today has about 1.6 billion followers world-wide, of whom around

80 percent are Sunnis and the rest Shias along with a number of smaller denominations, all considered to be blasphemous by the Sunnis.

In the Middle-East the Sunnis are represented by Saudi Arabia, Qatar, Turkey and their allies while the Shias are championed by Iran, Lebanon and Syria. In this consideration, Iraq is not being included since it ceased to be a viable state after 2003 when the US invaded and destroyed the cohesiveness of the nation. In any case, Iraq's geographic borders were drawn by the League of Nations in 1920 and does not have any sanctity in the eyes of the various religious and tribal groups now fighting there for hegemony. The extremist religious groups involved in the multi-cornered conflict that currently encompasses erstwhile Iraq and Syria are only concerned with religious borders and not geographic or political ones.

Historical Background

The Republic of Yemen occupies the southern end of the Arabian Peninsula and is the second largest country in the region, sharing a land border only with Saudi Arabia to the north. Its largest city is Sana'a which is also the constitutional capital. Yemen is an ancient country and its history can be traced back to at least the 11th century B.C. if not earlier. *[For brevity in analysing the current situation, the ancient, medieval, and the Ottoman Empire history of the country is not being elaborated here.]*

Although the division of the nation into two parts—the northern highlands ruled by Imam Yahya Hamidaddin and the southern parts ruled directly by the Ottoman representative—was established as early as 1911, it was only after the departure of the Ottomans and the intervention of the British that a clear political divide between the two parts of Yemen emerged. In the 1930s attempts by the Saudis under Ibn Saud tried to capture the northern parts ruled by the Imam were unsuccessful. In the south, at the end of a prolonged struggle the British sovereignty over the Aden protectorate was recognised.

In the north, at the death of the ruling Imam Ahmad bin Yahya in 1962, a group of army officers attempted to seize power from the prince who had succeeded to the throne, starting the North Yemen Civil War. Saudi Arabia, Britain and Jordan supported the prince while Egypt provided financial and materiel assistance to the republican officers. After nearly six years of civil war, in 1968, the republicans defeated the monarchists and created the Yemen Arab Republic. On the British leaving Aden, once again after a protracted insurgency, South Yemen became known as the People's Democratic Republic of Yemen.

The two Yemeni nations did not share a cordial relationship, blowing hot and cold, and even fighting a war in 1972. After an Arab League brokered peace deal, which included a declaration that unification would take place sometime in the future, Ali Abdallah Saleh became the President on North Yemen. *[For ease of understanding, the two countries will be referred to as North and South Yemen in this narrative.]* Sporadic fighting continued between the two countries till in 1986, a full-fledged civil war broke out in South Yemen. In 1990, the two governments reached an agreement for full reunification, merging officially on 22nd May with Saleh as the president. The then president of South Yemen, Ali Salim al-Beidh, became the vice president of the unified country.

The 1991 Gulf War was a watershed moment in the new country's brief history. President Saleh opposed the US-led intervention. Yemen was a member of the UN Security Council during 1990-91 and voted against the resolution permitting the 'use of force' against Iraq. In retaliation, Saudi Arabia expelled over 800,000 Yemenis living in the kingdom, which created immense socio-economic problems in Yemen. By 1993 the coalition was fractured and Vice President al-Beidh withdrew to Aden in protest, refusing to be part of a Government that he declared as being partisan. The result was the commencement of yet another desultory civil war that simmered with the military also functioning along the North-South divide. In 1994, the forces of South Yemen were defeated, although they were being supported by Saudi Arabia, and their leadership went into exile.

President Saleh continued to rule, almost as a dictator, and became the first directly elected president of Yemen in 1999, winning 96.2 per cent of the vote. Although a US naval ship, the *USS Cole*, was subjected to a suicide attack while in the port of Aden in October 2000, President Saleh assured US President George W. Bush that Yemen was a partner in the 'War on Terror' after the September 11 attacks in New York.

By June 2004, Shia insurgency had started to gain ground in Yemen with the dissident cleric Hussein Badreddin al-Houthi, head of the Zaidi Shia sect launching an uprising to 'defend their community against discrimination'. *[As an interesting aside, President Saleh also belonged to the same Shia sect.]* President Saleh won another term in the elections held in September 2006, but this time gaining only 77.2 per cent of votes. In the meantime the Shia uprising gradually gathered momentum—with suicide bombings becoming increasingly frequent throughout 2007-2009. In 2009, the Yemeni army, now actively assisted by Saudi Arabian forces, launched a crackdown against the Shia insurgents. Tens of thousands of people were displaced and although a ceasefire was brought about in February 2010, fighting continued, with the Zaidis (the fighting element calling itself Ansar Allah) accusing Saudi Arabia of providing support to Salafist groups engaged in suppressing Shias.

In January 2009, the Saudi and Yemeni al-Qaeda branches merged to form Al-Qaeda in the Arab Peninsula (AQAP) with a membership predominated by Saudi nationals. The activities of the AQAP prompted attacks—cruise missiles from fighter aircraft and subsequently missiles from uninhabited aerial vehicles—by the US, primarily targeted at AQAP leadership. There have been civilian casualties, unavoidable collateral damage in these strikes that have generated protests by human-rights groups.

Contemporary Developments

Under the long and autocratic rule of President Saleh, Yemen gradually turned into what can only be described as a kleptocracy. By 2009, it lacked strong State institutions and the government was overwhelmed by the need to balance a complex mix of tribal, regional, religious, and political interests. Power was shared between three men—the President, Ali Abdulla Saleh; Major General Ali Mohsen al-Ahmar who controlled a majority faction of the army; and Sheikh Abdullah al-Ahmar a figurehead leader of the Islamist Islah party and Saudi Arabia's chosen broker for the distribution of its financial largesse. Saudi Arabia relied on its financial clout to keep various tribal chieftains under its control. It is clear that the Saudi financial assistance was intended to directly influence the tribes and to keep them at least partially autonomous and away from Yemeni government influence. With this elaborate network creating an underlying influential layer it was possible for Saudi Arabia to have a 'proxy' say in Yemen's internal affairs.

It was inevitable that Yemen follow the Arab Spring revolutions and by March 2011 pro-democracy uprisings became common, catalysed by a move by Saleh to amend the constitution to facilitate his son inheriting the presidency. President Saleh's attempts at putting down the uprisings by force drew international condemnation and in November he flew to Riyadh to sign the GCC plan for political transition. The plan legally transferred the office and power of the president to the Vice President Abd Rabbuh Mansur Hadi. Hadi then won an uncontested election in February 2012 for a two year term and formed a 'unity' government that included the opposition.

The interim government conferred immunity on Saleh and about 500 of his associates, which led to thousands of people coming out on to the streets in protest. Although a National Dialogue Conference was launched in March 2012 to reach a consensus on the major issues facing the nation, no progress has so far been made. In January 2014, Hadi's term was extended by one year by the Conference. During this period AQAP was active in the country, carrying out effective suicide attacks against the government and the army. By early 2012, there was a US military presence in terms of Special Forces in Yemen to respond to AQAP activities. However, the Sana'a government continued to be weak, unable to face challenges from southern separatists, the AQAP and the Shia rebels. The political transition process was effectively held back by sectarian clashes between the Islah party and the Houthis.

Civil War

2014 saw the intensification of the Sunni-Shia conflict with the AQAP continuing its insurgency sporadically. In September 2014, the Houthis took over Sana'a and Ali Mohsen al-Ahmar, the de-facto leader of the Sunni faction, had to flee the country to Saudi Arabia. President Hadi was forced to accept a 'unity government' although the Houthis then refused to participate in the government. Subsequently, in February 2015, they placed the President under house arrest and dissolved the parliament, declaring a Revolutionary Committee under Mohammad Ali al-Houthi as the interim ruling authority in Yemen. This takeover, declared on 6th February was condemned by a number of foreign governments and, more importantly, by the United Nations. On 21st February President Hadi fled from Sana'a to Aden, his hometown and stronghold in the south. He declared Aden as the temporary capital and called for recognition as the constitutional president of Yemen.

Following the Houthi takeover several Western countries have closed their embassies in Sana'a while some Gulf countries, led by Saudi Arabia, have moved their embassies to Aden in a tacit move to legitimise Hadi's claim. The Houthis in the meantime have continued to move south and now surround Aden. A fallout of the Shia uprising has been that the US counter-terrorism operations have been wound down, with all the Special Forces in-country being evacuated on 22nd March. By this time the Houthi forces had captured the international airport in Aden after fierce fighting. The Houthi forces represent a fundamental change in the balance of power in the Arabian Peninsula, effectively creating an opportunity for Iran to become an influential actor in Yemen, which Saudi Arabia until now had considered their private backyard.

It is interesting to note that the rise of the Houthis was the result of miscalculations, primarily by Saudi Arabia and only indirectly influenced by the actions of the Yemeni government. There are three elements to this development, First, the Saudi attempt at putting down the Arab Spring-related uprisings backfired when Hadi took over as President. For years Saudi Arabia had supported the infighting within the several Yemeni factions in an effort to keep them divided and weak. The Houthis were able to take advantage of this dysfunctional situation and bring sufficient number of tribes under one fold to create the momentum to come out of their northern stronghold in strength.

Second, Riyadh was preoccupied with a number of challenges that arose almost simultaneously—combating AQAP; containing the fallout from the revolutions of the Arab Spring; stemming the security issues associated with the arrival of transnational jihadi groups to the area; and assisting Bahrain in putting down a Shia-led democratic uprising. While engaged in these multifarious efforts Saudi Arabia did not anticipate the rapid rise of Iranian influence in Yemen. The fact that the Zaidis are not a traditional Shia group may also have played a part in their ignoring the factional fight in Yemen.

Third, Saleh returned to Yemen, an event that should have been prevented by Saudi Arabia. Not only did his return and subsequent pardon trigger yet another violent demonstration, he was actively involved in undermining the Hadi government whom he blamed for his own earlier downfall. This exacerbated the simmering fissures that already existed along tribal, political, religious and military lines, making it almost impossible for the interim government to function effectively. The Government was unable to control and even worse incapable of influencing the political developments to stop the Houthi insurgency from rising.

What Now?

The future prospects for Yemen look worrying, to state it mildly. The political and military developments are one side of the coin, while the humanitarian aspect forms the other side. It has been predicted that at least half the people of Yemen already face food insecurity and water crisis, and that the population expected to double within the next 20 years. There are dire predictions that Sana'a will become dry of any usable water by as early as 2017. Oil production that provided 75 per cent of the government revenue has reduced to a trickle because of the civil war and it is once again being predicted that by 2017 oil production will stop making any meaningful contribution towards the national revenue. To cap these domestic woes, Saudi Arabia will suspend its multi-billion dollar aid program to protest the Houthi take over. The stage is set for another humanitarian debacle to unfold.

Foreign Intervention

It was always apparent that the Sunni-led GCC, particularly Saudi Arabia, would not stand by and watch Yemen being taken over by an Iran-supported Shia group. When it became clear that the Houthi forces intended to clear the entire country of Sunni influence, the Saudi-led coalition took action, launching a military campaign called 'Operation Decisive Storm'. It could be said that GCC has no choice but to take action. However, the unknown in this case is what Iran would do, since the Houthi forces have been fully supported and equipped by Iran from the beginning of their inception.

At the operational level, the Saudi-led intervention seems to be based on a similar concept to the war being fought against the Islamic State (IS) in Iraq and Syria—an air war to degrade and thereafter, hopefully, defeat the insurgents. However, there is a significant difference—the Saudis have not ruled out a ground offensive unlike the case of the US-led coalition against the IS. Perhaps this difference underlines the higher stakes that Saudi Arabia understands rides on the outcome of this conflict. It cannot afford to fail in Yemen. Essentially the proxy wars of influence that the Saudis have been waging for some time against Iran has now come out in the open. The outcome will decide the future of the monarchy in Saudi Arabia. The US and other major Western nations have voiced support for the military action with the US promising logistical and intelligence support. At the base level the military operation has added another layer of unpredictability and confusion to the Middle-East, which has now become one large war zone.

The Houthi 'rebels', initially a simple group from the north, have now become a major military presence and a politically active entity controlling almost the entire country. At the beginning of their campaign against the government in Sana'a the links to Iran was tenuous at best. However, Iranian support has become increasingly apparent and Iranian authorities have openly admitted that the Iranian Revolutionary Guards elite Qods Force has been training Houthi combatants in both Yemen and Iran. On 20th March an Iranian ship docked at a Houthi-controlled port and unloaded 180 tons of weapons and ammunition.

The stage is set for a direct confrontation between the Shia group led by Iran and the Sunnis led by Saudi Arabia. This is the age-old conflict that has come back to haunt the Middle-East. All other past conflicts that have taken place in the region pale into insignificance in front of the brewing war.

A Saudi-Iran Confrontation—The Changing Balance of Power

The sudden arrival of the Houthis into the mainstream political process in Yemen was more the result of the infighting in the political leadership than any premeditated action by the Houthi leadership. The Saudi decision to undermine the influence of the Muslim Brotherhood in Yemen lest their influence spread to Saudi Arabia also aided the rise of the Houthis. By the time the Houthis decided to oppose the government's decision to cut fuel subsidies that led to street protests and riots, there was no viable opposition to reign in their organised onslaught. Even some of the military units actively assisted in the Houthi takeover of the capital Sana'a. The takeover of the capital and fleeing of the President were catalysts for evolving a movement that was primarily created to safeguard the Zaidi tradition into becoming an alternative government by consolidating its military and political potential. This transformation made it necessary for the Houthis to involve themselves in security, administration and other State institutions. The trappings of a government were thrust on them, and accepted, even if reluctantly.

The real political agenda of the Houthis is still subject to speculation with their adversaries accusing them of attempting to usher in an Iran-supported Shia 'revolution', which is part of Iran's broader ambition of creating greater geopolitical influence for itself. Ansar Allah, the fighting element of the Houthi movement, can be considered an organisation wedded to the concept of restoring the nation's security; fighting the AQAP; and defending national sovereignty. In what is a fundamental divergence from other radical and militant groups, Ansar Allah has attempted to publicise documents that prove Saudi bribes to Yemeni politicians for years and the complicity of the high ranking personalities of the previous regime with AQAP and radical Salafists. Ansar Allah remains an enigma in an otherwise predictable landscape of extremist groups! To be unbiased and fair, it must be accepted that the Houthis are not the fundamental cause of sectarian polarisation in Yemen, but a reaction to it.

The situation is ripe for the Saudi-Iran proxy fight to come out in the open. The question is whether or not Iran is reckless enough to intervene openly and with sufficient ferocity to take the Arab intervention to the next level of open conflict with the Saudis and their allies. It is obvious that Iran is measuring its strategic influence in the region. They understand that had it not been for the rapid spread of IS, Bashar al-Assad would not have been permitted to continue in partial power in Syria. His fall would have been a definitive defeat for Iran's regional policies. The other Iran protégé, the Hezbollah in Lebanon, is not in as strong a position as Iran would have liked it to be.

Within Iraq and Syria where the IS is being fought, Iran already controls territory directly and through its militia agents, and has established its influence through financial and spiritual support. However, Iran is pragmatic enough to accept that a Syria ruled by Assad is not a viable end-state anymore. Further, the emergence of the IS as a strong Sunni force has unnerved Iran. Its long-term calculations seem to have gone somewhat awry in the past few months. The only consolation is that the Saudi calculations in terms of support for Sunni extremist groups have fared even worse. The IS, a Sunni entity, poses a direct threat to Saudi Arabia. However, this does not ease the Iranian situation and it is difficult to miss the extreme sectarian undertone in all Iranian activities. Syria is almost completely controlled by Iran and Bashar al-Assad is only a figurehead.

Iran's enterprise in Yemen must be viewed through this slight constraint within which Iran is currently functioning. Iran controls the activities of the Houthi element through its financial, materiel, and spiritual support. However, the rising power of the Houthis have send out a wake-up call to the GCC nations. The Iranian threat is now staring them in the face. Military action under these circumstances was a foregone conclusion.

Conclusion

The on-going conflicts in the Middle-East are multi-dimensional and the strategic scenario is extremely confusing in terms of alliances and cooperation. Scenario 1: the US backs the Saudi-led coalition in Yemen that is fighting the Iranian-backed Houthis/Ansar Allah; the US is also aligned along with the Iranian-backed militias in Iraq and Syria against the IS. Scenario 2: Egypt and the UAE are bombing Turkey and Qatar backed faction in Libya; all four of these nations work together in the Saudi-led coalition against Iran in Yemen. In Syria, the absolute base instincts and nature of all the nations can be seen while they compete nakedly for influence.

Saudi Arabia and its allies have firmly declared that their military operation, aimed at restoring the control of the 'legitimate' government of Hadi, is fundamental to the stability of the region. This may indeed be so, when viewed from Saudi Arabia's and the GCC's perspective. However, the military intervention in Yemen also demonstrates the abject failure of Saudi Arabia's decades old initiatives. Saudi Arabia exported the fundamental Wahabi strain of Sunni Islam around the globe through direct and indirect support to terrorist groups. These groups have now morphed into al-Qaeda and the IS, threatening the very existence of the Arab kingdom itself. The turkeys are now coming home to roost. On the other hand, post the 1979 revolution, the Iranian theocracy has also provided unconditional support to the Shia majority nations and to Shia-oriented rulers. Their steadfast approach has culminated in a slightly more reliable support base in comparison to the results achieved by Saudi Arabia. For the Saudis Yemen exemplifies a humiliating culmination of expanding Iranian influence in the Middle-East. They view the events in Yemen as the epitome of diminishing Sunni influence in the region and will not let it take hold. A change in the balance of power is unavoidable.

Ever since King Salman took over the reins of the country, Saudi Arabia has engaged in frantic diplomacy to cement a Sunni coalition that would be willing to carryout military action against Iranian backed Shia encroachment or attempts at further spreading Shia influence. These Sunni powers would also include Turkey, Egypt and Pakistan along with other Arab nations. With the launch of Operation Decisive Storm, the Saudis are giving notice that any further expansion of Iranian influence will not be tolerated. It is also a statement that they will not wait for the US to protect their interests. The military intervention is really not about Yemen or its future, but a counter strategy to push Shia influence away and stop the Sunni Yemenis from joining hands with the AQAP and IS.

The Saudis seem to have decided that it is time for a showdown with Iran. On whether or not Iran will pick up the gauntlet will depend the future of the most impoverished Arab country—Yemen— now unwittingly being forced to become the Arab gladiatorial arena.

Published on 4 April 2015 in Blog **sanukay.wordpress.com**

3

YEMEN
WHO IS FIGHTING WHOM, AND WHY?

All the nations of the Middle-East are now at war—against one another or against undefinable entities who are pursuing their own warped agenda—ruthlessly attempting to shore up lost prestige, struggling to retain power and influence, and to regain long lost command over the region. The rationale put forward is the necessity to ensure that the sovereignty of the nation is safeguarded. The underlying theme however is never mentioned openly—the struggle between Saudi Arabia and Iran through their respective proxy elements and allies, for political and religious domination of the region. This regional competition has now spilled over to the entire Islamic world, with shifting allegiances and short-term alienations being more common than the more prosaic, but understandable alliances.

The Middle-East defies definition—the fault lines between the Sunni and Shia sects of Islam are deeply etched in the sand and visible for all to see; while almost simultaneously the same lines are blurred into indistinct scratches, as self-serving and narrow national interests are brought to bear in an enforcement of realpolitik. The turmoil, so far considered as having been created and nurtured by Western nations against the Muslim world, has finally shown its true form. The conflict(s) in the Middle-East have now demonstrated that they are internal wars within the broader Islamic religion.

Yemen, and the raging conflict there, is a true example of this internal strife. Yemen, home to 25 million people, is the poorest nation in the Middle-East. It is a nation with an exploding population, where unemployment is above 40 percent, and water is scarce. Yemen is also fragmented—divided between the rich and more populous south and the poorer and mountainous north; and riven by a myriad of clans, tribes and familial bands at odds with each other. Until 1990, it was not even a unified nation and even after unification fought a destructive fratricidal civil war in 1994. The Houthis, a northern tribe, fought six separate wars with the government between 2004 and 2013 without much success till they turned the tables in the current iteration of the conflict.

There are three primary participants in the current chaos: the Iranian-supported Houthi rebels; the Saudi Arabia-led Sunni Arab coalition; and the al-Qaeda in the Arab Peninsula (AQAP). On the sidelines—cheering on the conflict is the United States; caught on a cleft stick is Pakistan; and aspiring to play an influential role in the nation's affairs is the ousted, but previously long-serving president of Yemen, Ali Abdullah Saleh.

The Houthis

The Houthis are a fundamentalist Shia group, taking their name from Hussein Badreddin al-Houthi, who launched a revolution against the government in 2004 and was killed by the Yemeni army later that year. The group has very clear objectives, which are spelt out on their flag in five statements, the first and the last in green colour—'God is Great; Death to America; Death to Israel; Curse on the Jews; Victory to Islam'. *[This is a translation taken from an op-ed published on 11 April 2015 and maybe at slight variance in a nuanced manner with some other translation of the slogan. However, the absolute clarity of their mission objectives cannot be denied.]*

Even after the death of their leader, the Houthis have continued the uprising with the financial and materiel support of the Qud force of the Iranian Revolutionary Guard for the past decade. Further, they are also in alliance with a part of the Yemeni military/security forces who are still loyal to the ousted president, Abdullah Saleh. This military group is reported to be in full control of the Yemeni Air Force. The Houthis have overrun the capital Sana'a and control large parts of the country, while the incumbent president, Abd Rabbuh Mansur Hadi is in self-imposed exile in Saudi Arabia.

One important factor is that although the Houthis are Shiites, they are of the Zayidi clan, one that is not universally recognised as main stream Islam even in Iran. On the one hand, the Houthi rebellion can hardly be considered religious, it is more about control of their own destiny. On the other, the Arab coalition has tried to simplify a complex situation by labelling the Houthi uprising an Iranian-controlled effort. This is patently incorrect; yes, the rebellion is supported by the Iranian regime, but the Houthi agenda is completely their own—they are home-grown and their roots in Yemen go back thousands of years. They are highly unlikely to completely toe Iran's instructions now or into the future.

Without doubt the Houthi fighters have friendly relations with Iran, but the driving force behind the Houthis come from within Yemen. The fact that they also represent a very large and entrenched social and political movement with popular and national support within the country is the most important factor that sustains the Houthis. This mass support has been garnered because of two fundamental reasons—the visible failure of the government to deliver succour and the alliance of a large part of the Yemeni army with the Houthis.

The Saudi-led Arab Coalition

Unable to condone the increasing Iranian influence in Yemen any further, Saudi Arabia decided to support the beleaguered President Hadi by launching an air campaign against the Houthi rebel movement. This intervention was endorsed by a subsequent Arab League summit and ten Arab nations have united under the Saudi-led coalition banner to create an 'Arab Army' dedicated to restoring President Hadi to power through defeating the Houthi Group and stopping them from taking over Yemen. This coalition is actively supported and encouraged by the USA and UK.

The coalition accuses Iran of using the Shiite Houthi movement as their proxies, and represents the crisis as a clash between Iran and Arab nations, part of the on-going Sunni-Shia tensions in the Middle-East and elsewhere in the Islamic world. On another level however, the conflict is in reality the extension of a long running conflict over control of political power and resources, not fundamentally about religion. It could even be envisaged that the sectarian violence is the result of Saudi intervention and not the cause.

So far the coalition has only used air power and naval artillery to attack Houthis, destroying arms caches and temporarily halting the Houthi advance in the south. There are reports that despite the four-week long bombing campaign, the Houthis are making progress into Southern Yemen, forcing the US to increase logistical support and intelligence sharing with the Arab coalition. Before the military intervention, Yemen was already in crisis in multiple areas, the air campaign has only made the situation more complicated. The intervention is almost completely against the cautious and discretionary approach that Saudi diplomacy and foreign policy has taken in the past few decades. Under these circumstances, there are questions looming regarding the maturity of the current, and much younger, Saudi leadership and the reasons for the rapidity with which the intervention was commenced.

So what was the motivation for the intervention? There is one viewpoint that the military operation was a reaction to a perceived and/or actual and immediate security threat posed to the Saudi kingdom by the turmoil in Yemen. It is pointed out that a Shia dominated Yemen will be a security threat to the entire region, especially at the strategic straits of Bab-el-Mandel. This is the argument being put forward by the Saudi government and its spokespersons in both regional and international arenas. However, the argument is not substantiated in a detailed analysis. First, the Saudi military machine is far too superior to the capabilities that the Houthis can bring to bear on the battlefield. Second, the Houthis do not have the ability to threaten the Bab-el-Mandel straits, especially when major maritime powers are present in the region and there is clear understanding that the safety of international shipping is directly connected to global economic security. It is noteworthy that in the past few days the US Navy has positioned the strike-group led by the aircraft carrier *Theodore Roosevelt* to ensure maritime security in the region.

Perhaps more importantly, the current crisis in Yemen is the outcome of the failed policies adopted, primarily by Saudi Arabia, towards Yemen in the past few decades. This conclusion is based on the fact that the 2011 uprising in Yemen failed to deliver any tangible improvement to the lives of the common Yemeni people. The change of leadership, from Saleh to Hadi, was ornamental at best. The Arab rhetoric of blaming Iran for the current conflict is to be seen and understood as just that, empty rhetoric. The path that the Houthis have followed to gain the current power and influence in the nation should have been recognised by the Arab governments and dealt with through political accommodation at a much earlier stage. On the contrary, military intervention has completely weakened any chances of a political compromise with the Houthis and led to escalation of the crisis.

Viewed in an overarching manner, it would seem that the military intervention was primarily aimed at rebuilding Saudi Arabia's prestige and influence in the region and to bolster its status in international forums. The fact that this was a unilateral Saudi decision, at least outwardly taken devoid of consultation with the US, emphasises the point further. The reasoning of threat to Saudi security and territorial integrity as being projected is difficult to believe. There is little doubt that the new Saudi leadership was less than happy with the decreasing influence of the nation in the region and blamed the diminishing status on the nation's old foreign policy that was fundamentally based on religious lead as the 'Custodian of the Two Holy Mosques' and economic might that stems from oil exports. Employing the nation's billion-dollar military in a mighty and brutal show of force was the demonstration of another aspect of national power as a proof of intent and will. Yemen was the obvious choice for this unilateral action, since it was felt that military intervention in the backwaters that Yemen is would not elicit a great deal of regional or international comment or condemnation.

It can also be speculated that by seeking a military solution in Yemen, Saudi Arabia is setting the scene to increase its influence in other conflicts currently underway in the region, particularly in Syria. If the Houthis are decimated militarily and forced to accept a political settlement that favours President Hadi and returns him to power, then it could be used as a lever to diminish Iranian influence. In turn this could force the removal of Bashar al-Assad, which is a fundamental objective of the Saudi establishment. Viewed dispassionately, this is a huge and convoluted gamble on the part of the Saudi monarchy. The reinstatement of President Hadi, which has not happened so far, and is unlikely to take place in the near term, is the one event that Saudi Arabia would be fervently hoping for at the moment. The domestic consequences of failure to achieve this stated objective for the Saudi leadership is far too severe to contemplate.

It is still early days to fully understand the consequences of Saudi Arabia's military enterprise in Yemen and it is still not clear whether the action has boosted Saudi prestige in the eyes of the onlookers. However, the chances of changing the political equation in Yemen and restoring Hadi to the 'throne' purely through air strikes is diminishing daily. More than anyone else, the Saudis are aware of this. This is the reason for the Saudis to have announced a 'new phase' in the Yemen operation, even changing the name from 'Operation Decisive Storm' to 'Operation Renewal of Hope'. Along with this change of name, the military objectives to be achieved have been listed. Obviously this is the first step towards arriving at a negotiated settlement. The sticking point in this process could well be the role of Iran.

Even if a lengthy and messy military operation is carried out, the civil war in Yemen will defy a military solution. It is common knowledge that once wars are initiated, they tend to take a life of their own and every single action can have unexpected repercussions and consequences. In the current situation it is to be hoped—for the sake of some semblance of stability in the Middle-East—that this military adventure will not blow up in Saudi Arabia's face.

AQAP

AQAP is a spin-off al Qaeda group formed in 2009 and led by Nasser al-Wuhayasi, a former aide to Osama Bin Laden. This is a totally Sunni organisation but its objective is to topple the Saudi monarchy (also Sunni) and also the Yemeni government (irrespective of who controls Yemen) in order to establish an Islamic Caliphate in the Arabian Peninsula. The AQAP therefore opposes both the Houthi movement as well as President Hadi, a Sunni Muslim. They also face opposition from the nascent Yemeni affiliate of the Islamic State, although the IS is also trying to establish an Islamic Caliphate. The difference between the two is in the severity of the practice of the religion that the groups advocate, which has become an unbridgeable gap between the two essentially Sunni groups. The IS is against everyone, except itself—they oppose the Houthis, the Sunni president, the AQAP and the anti-Houthi Sunni alliance led by Saudi Arabia. If ever there was confusion regarding alliances, this is it.

Even with the rise of IS as a primary threat to the Middle-East, the US government has continued to regard AQAP in Yemen as the most severe terrorist threat to the US. The current focus in Yemen—for the Sunni Arab coalition and its mentor the US—is the defeat of the Shia Houthis. The success of the Saudi-led military action in stopping the advance of the Houthis has also created an increase in the chaos on the ground. The result has been greater space for the AQAP to strengthen itself and expand its influence. This will have two foregone consequences—one that the competition between the AQAP and the IS will intensify; and two, that this struggle for supremacy will spill over into terrorist actions abroad as a means of demonstrating their competence to would-be supporters. In both cases, the people of Yemen will be the losers.

The Role of the United Sates – Cheer Leaders?

The US involvement in Yemen is longstanding and dates back to the Carter administration in 1979. According to some sources, at that time the CIA funnelled money to King Hussein of Jordan to foment a north-south civil war in Yemen. It is no secret that US Special Forces have been on the ground for the past decade, directing UCAV strikes. They had to beat a hasty retreat when the Houthi rebellion gained momentum, setting back the US fight against AQAP.

The Saudi-led military action in Yemen shows up the paradoxes and logical disconnects that exemplifies US policy in the Middle-East. It also demonstrates the unwillingness of the US policy-making community to learn from their past mistakes and their willingness to attempt the proven impossible yet again. The US Middle-East policy, at least at the current moment, seems to be the eternal circle with no beginning and no end. First there is the pattern of US military support. The US support to the Shah of Iran was almost absolute and when the current Shiite Islamist government overthrew the monarchy in 1979, they also got hold of all the US supplied weapons, which were sophisticated and at the cutting edge of technology for that time. In the 1980s the US supported the Mujahedeen fighting the Soviet occupation of Afghanistan and when they morphed into al Qaeda, they continued to use the US-supplied weapons. More recently, the Iraqi forces that vanished in the face of the IS onslaught also left the US weapons for the IS to capture and use.

Second, the US has been meddling in the Middle-East for decades, much prior to any terrorist attack on US mainland. Since the attacks on the twin towers in September 2001, the US has attacked or invaded seven Muslim nations. Although both Presidents Bush and Obama categorically state that the US is not at war with Islam, it is convenient for the extremist Muslim fringe to convince their followers that this claim is patently incorrect. They believe that the US is waging war on Islam. The paradoxes do not end there. The US is supporting the Saudi-led Arab coalition in Yemen—with materiel, intelligence and maritime sanitisation of strategic sea lines of communication—because the Houthis are clearly allied with Iran and opposed to the Yemeni government whose support is essential for the US to continue its war against AQAP, which is considered a priority in the US policy team. However, blanked out in this calculation is the fact that the Houthis themselves are perhaps the strongest enemies of the AQAP. On the other side of the Middle-East, in

Iraq and Syria, the US is tacitly cooperating with Iran to fight the IS. How does this align with the actions in Yemen? It does not. So the US continues to muddy the Middle-Eastern waters through shifting allegiances and promises of friendships.

Perhaps this confusion in US foreign policy is the result of a very fundamental streak in the American character that makes them believe that in a two-sided conflict, one side is good and the other bad and that the US should always support the 'good' side. However, in this manifestation, the fact that the decision of who is good and who is bad is made purely by American perceptions is almost always forgotten. That this situation leads to confusion would be an understatement. The IS imbroglio is a good example. The US is allied with Iran in the fight against IS; in Syria, the US supports groups who oppose the regime (and is therefore considered to be the 'good' guys) while the regime is also fighting the same IS and the local al Qaeda affiliate. The situation cannot get more chaotic.

Pakistan – Caught in a Cleft Stick

Although the Middle-Eastern monarchies have armies that are equipped with the latest weapons, they have almost always looked outside the Middle-East—primarily to Egypt and Pakistan—to bolster their forces in times of conflict. The reasons for this are—the tribal composition of the Arab armies; a less than optimal training regime as compared to the Western forces; and most importantly, the fact that the Arab armies have not been battle-tested for the past two decades or more. This was the reason for the Saudis making a direct call to Pakistan, which has an experienced army at its disposal, to join the coalition with both air and land power. In fact the announcement was made that Pakistan was part of the coalition immediately after King Salman spoke to Prime Minister Nawaz Sharif, even before any formal answer was provided; a clear indication of the strategic clout that Saudi Arabia thought it had over Pakistan.

There is no doubt that Pakistan is beholden to Riyadh, but the Pakistani generals are extremely concerned about their national security and the Army is in the middle of a protracted campaign in the tribal region of the country. Pakistani declining to be drawn into the Yemeni conflict on the request for military participation was a great shock to the Saudi monarchy. Initially the Islamabad government demurred; then they turned over the request to the

Parliament; and that august body, after much heated debate, declined to send its military forces to aid their long-term benefactor. The parliament's decision was hard-hearted and based purely on calculations done in the head. Pragmatism had won over sentiments.

It is simple to see why the Gulf Sheikhdoms and the Kingdom of Saudi Arabia took the participation of Pakistan in the Yemen conflict for granted. In particular the Saudi largesse and the particularly close relationship that Nawaz Sharif has cultivated with the Saudi monarchy is open to public view. In 1998, when Pakistan under the first prime ministership of Sharif, carried out nuclear testing, the Saudis softened their sanctions; oil worth billions of dollars was provided to Pakistan on deferred payments and free for five years *[although this facility was later revoked when General Pervez Musharraf took over as military dictator]*; it hosted the entire Sharif family lavishly when they were in exile and assisted the setting up of multi-million dollar enterprises for the family; and they ensured that he would not be deported again on returning to Pakistan by sending him back in a Royal Saudi aircraft. In providing unstinting support to Nawaz Sharif, the Saudi's were making a calculated investment. The Yemen conflict was payback time.

In 2014, when the Pakistani Rupee was on the verge of sinking, US $ 1.5 billion was deposited mysteriously in Pakistan's Central Reserve Bank, the donor is easy to identify! Doubtlessly, there were few Pakistanis at that time who questioned the wisdom of accepting such enormous 'gifts', but were silenced by the Government's declaration that there was no quid pro quo. Obviously this was not true.

The denial of military aid itself was a hard hit to absorb for the Saudi monarchy, but rubbing salt on a fresh wound, the Parliament also declared that, '…[the Parliament] desires that Pakistan should maintain neutrality in the Yemen crisis…'. Almost as a last minute sop to the Saudis, the most powerful ally that Pakistan has ever had, it also declared that it would 'stand shoulder to shoulder' with Saudi Arabia if its territorial integrity is threatened directly. There is no doubt that the Saudis were dismayed. However, this is an instance of national self-interest superseding material and spiritual ties. There is no doubt that the Parliament's decision came as something of a surprise for Nawaz Sharif.

There are three reasons for the pragmatic Pakistani decision. One, the awareness of the extreme danger of taking sides in what is essentially a power struggle between Saudi Arabia and Iran. Two, a little more than 20 percent of Pakistan's population are Shias and already the nation is rife with sectarian violence. Three, and most importantly, Pakistan shares a 900-kilometer, porous land border with Iran. The Iranian Foreign Minister visited Pakistan recently and it can be assumed that he hammered home some hard-headed realities that should keep the Pakistani decision-makers on the straight and narrow path of self-interest. However, the Saudis also hold a trump card in their hands; Pakistani expatriates living in the kingdom remit more than US $ 8 billion annually, which represents half of the total of $ 16 billion in overseas remittances that clearly shore up a sagging economy. At the moment Pakistan sits between Scylla and Charybdis—Saudi Arabia and other Arab nations on one side and Iran on the other.

Pakistan has every right to be vary of joining another war. Its proxy involvement in regional wars, starting with the Mujahidin against the Soviet occupation of Afghanistan, has created extremely serious fractures in the State and society. The massive Saudi funding of seminaries have resulted in sectarianism led by murderous Sunni attacks on the Shia minority. Radical Islam has spread across the societal structure and now threatens to engulf the nation with religious intolerance. The Taliban now has a stranglehold in some of the more restive parts of the country. The society is divided and Pakistan has effectively become the ideological battleground between Saudi Arabia and Iran. Taking sides at this juncture is perhaps the worst decision that the leadership could make.

Will this refusal trigger the start of a widening gulf between the Arab monarchies and Pakistan? While the changes to the cosy relationship that has so far been shared by the two sides cannot be explicitly determined now, the fact remains that Pakistan's refusal will certainly impact on future relationships. The UAE has already made this very clear. Saudi Arabia will in all likelihood bide its time and change the relationship only gradually. But change it will, and Pakistan should be under no other illusion.

Conclusion

As this is being written (27-30 April 2015) the Saudi-led coalition has declared a unilateral ceasefire in the air campaign and also broken it a few hours later. The air campaign continues in a slightly lesser intensity. They also declared that the focus has shifted from counterinsurgency to negotiations and humanitarian assistance. However, in less than 48 hours after the announcement, air strikes once again targeted Houthi bases and assembly points, suggesting that the reprieve was not sacrosanct. The decision to effect a ceasefire was perhaps based on the understanding that any other option would spiral out of control and draw the Arab forces into an unwinnable war of their own creation. The lessons of the 2008-09 border war that Saudi Arabia fought with the Ansar Allah the Houthi fighting force, in which the Saudi forces came out second best, has not been forgotten by the Saudi leadership. Therefore, although the ceasefire was violated almost immediately, it can be expected that there will be concerted attempts to make it work. The Houthis have also stated that they are amenable to a United Nations-sponsored peace talks once the air strikes have been fully discontinued. This has not happened as yet.

Middle-East media has claimed that 150,000 troops have been mobilised on the southern borders of Saudi Arabia and that a ground invasion could be launched if required. While the Kingdom has definitely demonstrated that it would resist the Houthis through its military action over the past few weeks, it is almost certain that the Saudis would avoid a ground war that could turn very ugly. However, Saudi Arabia's stated goal is to reinstate the now in exile President Hadi. If this cannot be achieved, either through military action or political dialogue and accommodation, it will be an embarrassing defeat for the nation. Failure carries its own price, especially for the young leadership at the helm in Saudi Arabia.

The signals from Saudi Arabia are unequivocal in seeking a negotiated solution. This would involve Hadi being returned to power and a peace agreement with, and between, the warring factions. Such a state would also involve a gradual increase in the autonomy of provinces through constitutional change, especially to stem the secessionist movement in South Yemen. However, what the Saudi Arabian monarchy wants and what they will get may not be mutually compatible and therein lies the crux of the peace deal. At the very fundamental level what Saudi Arabia wants is to keep Shiites outside its periphery and to ensure Sunni dominance of the region. Under the prevailing circumstances this may not be achievable in the absolute. Irrespective of the outcome of the military campaign, a political solution in which the Houthis have a significant say in matters of State is the only way a protracted low-intensity conflict can be avoided in Yemen. A low-intensity conflict would produce the ideal state in which the AQAP and IS would be able to operate with impunity and increase their already strong influence—a nightmarish scenario.

For the sake of the people of Yemen, it has to be 'hoped' that the new phase of coalition operations, aptly named 'Operation Renewal of Hope' will bring succour to them with no political strings attached. Perhaps a Utopian dream!

Published on 29 April 2015 in Blog sanukay.wordpress.com

4

BANGLADESH
BEING SWALLOWED BY INACTION

Ever since it's tumultuous birth in 1971, Bangladesh has been caught in an identity trap. The nation's linguistic, secularist and, most importantly, its religious identity have often been in conflict with each other, preventing the nation and the people from forging a clearly defined identity of its own. In fact the nation can claim the dubious honour of being the only country whose identity is based primarily on language, than on any other single factor. There are two elements that influence the politics of the country—one that it is a Muslim majority nation; and two, flowing from the first, that electoral politics do not permit anyone to take an unambiguous stance regarding the role of religion in the broader aspects of governing the State. Superimpose the historical evolution of the nation, at the time of the partition of India in 1947 being hived out of the larger Bengal State as a Muslim majority region as part of the newly created Pakistan, and the confusion is almost tangibly visible.

The vagueness of perception regarding religion is starkly reflected in the constitution that proclaims secularism and at the same time also acknowledges Islam as the state religion. This imprecise view of religion makes it difficult for a political party to completely eschew religion and declare itself a truly secular entity. It is through this lens that the recent spate of murders in the country have to be viewed. In less than three months, three 'bloggers' who posted liberal articles regarding religion or questioned the fundamentalist interpretation of Islam on their blogsites were hacked to death in public view by religious fanatics. They also happened to be on a list of 84 'liberals' that the Islamic fundamentalists have identified for elimination. The response from both the Government and the opposition to the murders have been muted; there have been no strong condemnation of these heinous crimes; there was no stridently visible outrage from normal citizens. What has happened to Bangladesh?

Historic Background

Bangladesh is a country of rivers, cyclones, and paddy fields; also of poets, artists, and patriots. Since restoration of democracy in 1991, after years of military dictatorial rule, Bangladesh has been alternatively ruled by the two major national parties—the Awami League (AL) and the Bangladesh National party (BNP). There are also a number of smaller parties that support or oppose the government dependent on their electoral alliance. The nation has a five-year electoral cycle and in 1996, all parties agreed to put in place a caretaker government to oversee the elections in a fair and free manner. However, this agreement was considered flexible and has undergone a number of amendments over the years. Further, even the electoral laws have been altered and token secularism formally introduced.

The system worked in a more or less equitable manner till 2006, when the BNP government, ruling in an alliance with Jamaat-e-Islami (JEI) a fundamentalist religious organisation, appointed a caretaker government blatantly biased in their favour. The elections were delayed and in 2008 the people soundly rejected the BNP-JEI combine, giving the AL a clear majority— they won 230 of the total 300 seats. The 2013 elections were boycotted by BNP and its allies because of objections to some amendments to the constitution that emphasised the secular nature of the country, which the AL had introduced. The JEI was banned from contesting the elections since it refused to confirm to the amendments in the constitution. The end result was that the AL was elected to government unopposed. The BNP once again in opposition leads a motley group of 20 parties.

The Current Situation

Being kept out of power is always an unpalatable situation for political parties, especially when their popularity is dependent on the largesse that can be spread when in power. Having been side-lined for a year through an election that it boycotted in January 2014, the BNP launched an anti-Government agitation on 6 January this year. The timing of the agitation could also have been prompted by the AL Government led by Shiekh Hasina initiating a number of criminal charges against the leader of BNP, Khalida Zia and a number of other senior leaders of the party. By the end of February the agitation had assumed a life of its own, becoming almost a terror campaign, led by the JEI that provides the street power to the BNP. It has degenerated into an open show of belligerence by the opposition, to an extent that they called for a transport blockade on 21 February, the International Language Day which is much revered by all people in Bangladesh.

In Bangladesh, as in most of South Asia, agitations tend to turn violent fairly rapidly since the people are extremely sensitive to domestic political issues and are also prone to be overtly emotional in their reactions. The BNP-sponsored agitation and blockade was no exception and by late-January, violence had already become a part of the agitation process. However, popular support for it faded when the Secondary School Certificate examinations had to be postponed because of the deteriorating law and order situation in the country. In addition, the agitation has been met by brute force by the Government, which is in no mood to compromise on its own political agenda. The opposition has a single-point agenda of regaining power and the Government is oblivious to the impact of the violence being perpetuated on the common people. The reasoning provided by both sides for the impasse and initiating inimitable actions has been illogical and can be viewed merely as a struggle for power.

Essentially, this is a no-holds barred battle between AL and BNP for control of the nation and has led to chronic political unrest. It has directly impacted the economy and led to huge losses. By the end of February, Bangladesh had reached a state of political stalemate. Although the US had tried to broker some sort of a peace between the two warring parties, it has not borne any fruit so far; and it is unlikely to do so considering the extremely chauvinistic stance that Bangladesh has regarding national sovereignty and foreign interference in domestic issues. The on-going violent rivalry between the two main political parties has been an impediment to the process of democratic institution building that has been slow to take effect in the nation even though democracy was restored in 1991.

An On-going Issue

It has been roughly estimated by a number of agencies that Bangladesh is home to around 100 terror groups, each with their own individual agenda. It is also proven that there is endemic money-laundering by the local banks of funds received from the Middle-East, both as donations as well as remittances by expat workers. More than 10 million Bangladesh citizens work in the Middle-East in a variety of jobs. Although the government is seeking external assistance to curb money-laundering, the initiative has so far only met with token success.

A fundamental issue facing the government is that a number of these terrorist groups question the independence of Bangladesh from Pakistan, achieved in 1971 based purely on linguistic and ethnic differences. This goes to the very heart of the existence of the nation as a sovereign entity. The fact that some Islamists have been tried and executed for crimes against the people during the popular uprising in 1971 has added fuel to the terrorist fire. The society is gradually being divided and Pakistan is actively aiding this division, as a revenge action for Bangladesh separating and declaring independence in 1971. India's active support for the struggle for independence in 1971 has always been a bitter pill for Pakistan to swallow, which blames India for the dismemberment of a unified Pakistan.

The BNP is currently at the head of the agitation. However, its power on the street—markedly oriented towards sectarian violence—stems from the JEI cadre. The violence has taken its toll on the common people in a number of ways and has marred the socio-political system as never before. The simmering antipathy towards the BNP is pointing towards a situation wherein the classic fallout of this current agitation could well be the fall from grace of the BNP and its gradual fadeout into oblivion. If such a development does take place, it would leave the JEI, an extremist organisation if there ever was one, as the main opposition in the country. Entrenched and strategically focused violence against secularist forces will be the result—a sad commentary for a nation that is steeped in the traditional cultural ethos of religious, ethnic and linguistic tolerance.

The public opinion is also divided regarding the rule of AL under Shiekh Hasina, especially since the country has come to an economic halt in the past few months because of the intransigent attitude of the two major parties to achieving a compromise solution to the political impasse. Decline in democratic values is inherently detrimental to economic growth and Bangladesh has proven it through its lack of performance in the economic field in the past few years. It has not been able to take advantage of the shift in economic power balance from Europe to Asia and the people are impatient with the tardiness of the politicians still bent on fighting for power with not a thought for the betterment of the nation. Political stability, or the lack of it, is an on-going issue that troubles Bangladesh. There is no doubt that only a strong, well-entrenched and stable social situation will improve the socio-economic condition of the people. The travails of mis-governance has made the general public regard the perceived 'good governance' in more authoritarian states as a better option than a failing democracy. This perception, if developed to its logical conclusion, may yet prove to be a double-edged sword and detrimental to the fledgling democratic traditions of the nation.

Emergence of Religious Fundamentalism

Bangladesh has always had a fringe minority of religious fanatics who were tolerated by the larger community that was made up of the more tolerant Sufi-oriented followers of Islam. However, in the past few decades, extremist and fundamentalist followers of the religion has become more assertive in their attitude and turned towards violence to express their demands to further Islamise the society. Their ultimate and declared aim is the establishment of a State based on the Sharia Law in Bangladesh. This has created an ideological rivalry between secular nationalists and the orthodox religious groups. The divide has been further exacerbated by the AL Government instituting an International Crimes Tribunal to try the collaborators of the 1971 war of independence. Currently Bangladesh is in the throes of an ideological battle between secularists and hard-line Islamists. The end-result will determine whether or not this fragile State will continue on its democratic journey.

The killing of the three bloggers by religious extremists is the first indication of the targeting of free thinking and also the first step towards the intimidation of common people. The public murders should be viewed as the beginning of a 'culture of impunity' on the part of Islamic extremist factions and the inability of the government to enforce law and order. The perpetrators were all madrasa students who, it is believed, had not even read the blog posts that were considered anti-Islam. The Islamic political parties now openly target anyone who criticises them or the Islamic religion as atheists or apostates who deserve to be killed. This overt threat to atheists is a sad turn in a country known for its peace and tranquillity; its cultural greatness; and the gentleness of its ethnic population. Reading between the lines it is easy to clearly see the concerted attempt to subvert and eventually convert the inclusive, gentle, and tolerant Sufi-influenced version of Islam long-practised in Bangladesh to the obscurantist model of Wahabi Islam that is both regressive and exclusive.

The madrasa students who perpetuated the killings were obviously 'brain-washed' to undertake the murderous activities by more 'senior' extremists with a much broader agenda.

There are three factors that assist the creeping culture of religious intolerance in Bangladesh. First, the government has assumed a very soft approach towards the various militant groups, especially the newly formed vigilante groups who are at the forefront of the on-going violence. These groups pretend that they are 'protecting' Islam from blasphemers and the government's reluctance to take severe action against them is indicative of a larger malaise. Second, the large number of militant groups make it difficult to pinpoint one entity as responsible for a particular anti-national and/or illegal activity, especially when multiple groups claim responsibility for the act. Third, the domestic political scene is becoming murkily polarised. The polarisation has assumed greater proportions ever since the war crimes tribunal was instituted.

The on-going violence, perpetuated in the guise of political protest, is actually well directed and coordinated attacks meant as the initial steps towards controlling the future orientation of Bangladesh and its official acceptance of fundamentalist religious ideals. The strategy of the fundamentalists can also be discerned. The first step is to polarise the nation, especially considering the inability of the government to act decisively against sectarian forces; then to intimidate the secular agencies; and finally to have the majority of the youth sufficiently radicalised through the madrasas to become the voice of the 'people'. The mushrooming of madrasas across the country and the economic weakness of the nation combine and play into this strategy. The JEI, at the forefront of this movement, already has a militant student wing called Islami Chhatra Sibhir that directly threatens the secular ethos of the entire student body. While the JEI and its Islamic allies are in the process of constructing a religious juggernaut, the government has tended to adopt a lofty attitude towards this increasing menace, merely calling it terrorism and initiating only punitive actions. There has been no dialogue of significance between the government and the opposition BNP. If ever there was a prize for an ignorant and ill-considered reaction to a primary threat to the well-being of the nation, the government reaction in Bangladesh will win hands down.

The Dubious Role of Pakistan

Soon after the BNP agitation took hold, the Bangladesh Government asked Pakistan to withdraw an official from its High Commission, after he was arrested for collusion with, and financing, terrorist elements who were perpetuating criminal activities both in Bangladesh and across the border in India. It is clear that Pakistan's ISI network operates from within the Pakistan High Commission in Dhaka, aiding and fomenting trouble in the streets of Bangladesh. The Pakistan Army has not forgotten the humiliating defeat that it suffered in the liberation of Bangladesh (erstwhile East Pakistan) in 1971. Since the Army continues to influence the affairs of State in Pakistan and remains unchecked in its activities within the country and abroad, even though the nation is nominally under a democratically elected government, it will continue to support activities meant to subvert the stability of Bangladesh.

There is a proven link between the ISI and JEI activists and also of the ISI use of Bangladesh territory to infiltrate terrorists into India. This was far easier under the BNP-JEI rule who closed their eyes to these activities and the current government's clamping down on free movement across the Indian border has not gone down well with the ISI. Further, since Pakistan is obsessed with India as an 'enemy', the improving India-Bangladesh relationship under the current government is also anathema to the ISI. Shiekh Hasina has managed to appease the Bangladesh Army, who has behaved at times as the final arbitrator in the future of the country, and has also turned towards India for assistance in stabilising the nation. India in turn appreciates the non-religious political ideology of AL and has clearly articulated its preference for an AL-led government in Bangladesh.

The security establishment in Pakistan has been colluding with extremist groups for decades, much to the detriment of its own integrity. The only way to redeem the situation would be for it to make a permanent break with this decades-long affair with the jihadists—for the good of Pakistan and a better future for Bangladesh.

India's Interest

India is in the process of asserting its position as a strategic power and attempting to assume a regional leadership role. While domestic political considerations impinge on realising this vision, the urge to thwart China's influence in South Asia is a cardinal principle guiding India's external dealings. In this context, Bangladesh which has common borders with seven restive Indian states in which China foments trouble on a regular basis, becomes an important piece of the larger picture. For India a friendly Bangladesh is a non-negotiable imperative to ensure peace and stability in the volatile North-East of the country. This was the primary reason for India having supported the elections in Bangladesh in 2013, while the opposition had boycotted it and in defiance of the US, which had expressed its discomfort with the single party election going ahead.

The current political impasse and the mayhem brought about through the BNP-led violent agitation makes the AL government look for greater support from India to normalise the situation. India and the US have different views and opinions regarding the direction that Bangladesh should take in furthering its democratic institutions. The US wants the country to establish and entrench a two-party system, similar to what prevails in the US. India on the other hand wants secularism imposed on the political system as a prerequisite for democratic development. The AL fits the bill, whereas the BNP-JEI combination clearly is theocratic in nature.

The Indian government under Prime Minister Narendra Modi has already passed the constitutional amendment bill to implement the long pending Land Boundary Agreement with Bangladesh. The Indian Prime Minister is also slated to visit Bangladesh in June, and if the current situation is anything to go by, an understanding on the Teesta water sharing treaty could also be forthcoming. It is significant that the West Bengal Chief Minster, Mamta Banerjee who was instrumental in the previous Manmohan Singh government shelving the agreement, has been invited to accompany the Prime Minster on this visit. With this background, it is expected that a number of agreements— ranging from transport to trade—will be signed between the two countries during this visit. This is important for Shiekh Hasina to bolster her credibility as a leader who can deliver improvements for the country since she has been constantly lambasted in local politics as an 'Indian stooge', mainly by the Islamist opposition.

Bangladesh is a proud nation, born out of one of the bloodiest civil wars in which thousands of Bangladeshi freedom fighters operated out of India and millions of refugees were accepted into Indian Territory. However, history alone does not make for mutual understanding when large volumes of water has flown down the Teesta, Brahmaputra and Padma Rivers. The nations need to work together in a transparent manner to address each other's concerns regarding security and economy for stability to be built in the region.

Where to from here?

The space in which free and liberal ideas flourish and inevitably come to fruition is shrinking fast in Bangladesh. The reasons are many and common to fledgling democracies across the world—governmental apathy and inaction that permit extremist forces act with impudence; the corrosion of socio-economic ideals brought about through the entrenchment of crony politics and corruption; unchecked persecution of freedom of speech and expression by official decree and extra-judicial groups; and the inability of the judiciary to remain independent or to have their writ adhered to by other elements of the government. By polarising the society on religious grounds and imposing an impossibly harsh writ on the functioning of the normal society, the Islamists seem to be gaining ground in Bangladesh. The focused targeting of free thinkers who express themselves in cyberspace is visible proof of the decline of a once robust culture of enlightenment and tolerance.

Democracy can only be sustained through the propagation and entrenchment of liberal values—freedom of speech, the right to dissent peacefully, the right to practice one's religion of choice, the right to be treated as an equal irrespective of caste, creed and colour. It is the State that should determine who are criminals and bring them to justice and not religious extremists who act as judge, jury and executioner all at the same time. Placating these vigilantes will be the first brick placed in bording up the concept of liberal democracy once and for all. Hopefully the peace-loving majority of the Bangladeshi population will wake up to the dangers that their nation faces, before they too get swept away—swallowed by inaction.

Published in Eurasia Review 10 June 2015

http://www.eurasiareview.com/10062015-bangladesh-being-swallowed-by-inaction-analysis utm_source=feedburner&utm_medium=email& utm_campaign=Feed%3A+eurasiareview%2FVsnE+%28Eurasia+Review%29

5

PAKISTAN
STUCK IN A CUL-DE-SAC

Pakistan, a state created in the name of Islam, is today divided along linguistic, ethnic, tribal and sectarian lines. It also claims to be the 'heart of Asia', making any observer want to ask, 'a wounded, bleeding heart?' While it is beset with domestic issues that directly threaten the well-being of the nation as a whole—unrest in Baluchistan; the on-going military operations in the Federally Administered Tribal Areas (FATA); and the rapidly increasing sectarian violence against minorities—Pakistan is attempting a rather bizarre re-invention of itself as a progressive Muslim nation. This attempt is reliant on the creation of a non-Muslim threat as a rallying point to focus the population away from domestic challenges. Accordingly Pakistan has drummed up the rhetoric of Indian intervention and the hidden hand of the Research & Analysis Wing (RAW), the external intelligence agency of the Indian Government in recent months. This is at best an ostrich-like approach to its own security and the very real threat of disintegration on sectarian and tribal lines.

A General Appraisal

Although Pakistan's officialdom vehemently and repeatedly denies it, there is no doubt in anyone's mind that Pakistan uses terrorism in different garbs as a tool of foreign policy, especially in its dealings with India and Afghanistan. Pakistan has always aided, abetted, facilitated and protected terrorists, dividing them into 'good' and 'bad' terrorists; the good being the groups that toes the line and does its bidding, and the bad being the ones that create inconvenient domestic disturbances. In doing so it has emerged as a master at playing the double game, a duplicity that the Bush administration was unable to fathom in the early days of the 'war against terrorism'. The Taliban resurgence in Afghanistan, on-going from around 2006, is completely Pakistan supported, being controlled by the Army and ISI through the Frontier Corps. There is no indication that Pakistan wants to, or is attempting to, reign in the active Taliban insurgency in Afghanistan.

The Yemen crisis was a wakeup call for the Pakistani Government and the Army. So far they had adroitly played the nations of the Middle-East to their advantage. However, when the call came from Saudi Arabia for military participation in the Arab coalition, the reality of the situation hit the establishment. Whatever the agony involved, Pakistan had to say a direct 'no' to its benefactor for two reasons. First, the sectarian nature of the Yemen conflict made it impossible for the Pakistani Parliament to endorse a Sunni-biased military intervention. Second the Army found that it had no spare capacity to deploy to the Middle-East when they were in the midst of an intense counter-insurgency operation in North Waziristan. After the denial Pakistan has tried desperately to make amends through intense diplomacy, but the pragmatists in government and the Army know that it will not be business as usual anymore with the major nations of the Middle-East. Even so, Pakistan is unwilling to take sides in the increasingly confused politics and developing crises of the Middle-East—the conflict against the Islamic State (IS); the Sunni-Shia sectarian fights; and the Saudi-Iran stand-off.

The current Nawaz Sharif Government is caught in a cleft stick; it needs the support of the military to stay in power while its political support stems from the right-wing, the madrasa establishment. The deteriorating internal security situation has forced the government to accept the upper hand of the military. However, this balancing act cannot be continued for the long-term and there is always the possibility of a popular backlash, contrived by the religious right. Even without a political crisis the drift of the civilian government could continue till the next elections, scheduled for 2018.

There is clear and unambiguous evidence of the emergence of a cleric-criminal nexus functioning against the minorities. A number of militant religious groups have been indirectly state supported since the 1980s and their persecution of the Shia, Christian and Hazara minorities has somewhat discomfited the government. The situation is exacerbated by the lethargy in dispensing justice and the absence of any witness or prosecution protection in terror-related cases that makes people wary of violent extremism within the criminal justice system.

Other than the domestic sectarian violence and terrorist threat, there are two major internal issues that keeps Pakistan in a turmoil—the unrest in Baluchistan and the Army involvement in governing the State.

The Baluchistan Issue

There has been a festering dissident movement demanding greater autonomy in Baluchistan for decades. However, the agitation intensified after the popular Baluch leader, Nawab Akbar Bugti, was killed in a military operation on 26 August 2006. The official government response to the agitation has been based on physical suppression. Baloch dissidents have been killed and dumped on the roadside or have 'vanished'. It is generally believed that government agencies are behind the killings, although these agencies have resorted to falsification of evidence to show that they were not involved. The Protection of Pakistan Ordnance (PPO) gives the Army a free hand and the power to arrest and detain any 'suspect'. More worryingly, it gives the Army the authority to shoot anyone committing, or 'likely to commit' any terror-related offences. This gives a carte blanche for the Army to pursue its own agenda in the region; the Frontier Corps, a para-military force, functions outside the law of the Baluch Government.

The Pakistan Supreme Court recognises the extra-judicial killings and have reprimanded the Government, which in turn pleads its inability and helplessness to stop them. Since the beginning of the dissident movement, it is estimated that the Pakistan Army and other government agencies have been responsible for 21,000 persons going 'missing'. The question of the missing persons in Baluchistan has become sensitive enough for the government agencies to now try and silence the media through a targeted and focused campaign of assassination. By all accounts, 30 journalists have so far been killed. A classic case was the murder of Sabeen Mahmud, a women's rights activist, in early May this year.

Baluchistan is resource-rich and the largest of Pakistan's four provinces, although it is sparsely populated with only seven million residents. Despite its vast natural resources, it is also Pakistan's poorest province. There are a number of Baluch 'Liberation' militant formations that are listed by the Baluchistan government as being anti-national and are being targeted as part of a 'smart and effective security policy'. Along with this, Islamabad has followed a strategy of supporting armed Islamic extremist militant groups that function as proxies of the State in the province. The situation has been purposely aggravated, almost like a smoke screen to cover up the extremely brutal suppression of Baluchi aspirations that is taking place on a daily basis. The tragic cycle of events—the killing of ethnic Baluchi people by the security forces and the retaliatory attacks on non-Baluchi residents—tells a story of Pakistan's repeated failures.

The Army – In a World of its Own

The Army has been carrying out Operation Zarg-e-Azb in North Waziristan, against the insurgents, since June 2014. The Tehreek-e-Taliban Pakistan (TTP) responded on 16 December 2014 with the infamous attack on the Army Public School in Peshawar in which 132 students were massacred. It is interesting that initially the operation was a unilateral Army decision with very reluctant civilian government support garnered after its commencement. However, the Peshawar school attack by the insurgents made it easier for politicians to support the on-going Army action. The terrorists unwittingly played into the hands of the Army by perpetrating this brutal and sadistic attack on school children.

The Army initiated and ratified a 20-point National Action Plan (NAP) to tackle terror, listing a number of initiatives with very 'noble' intent. One of the major initiative was the establishment of the Military Courts to try terrorists, facilitated through amending the Constitution as well as the 1952 Army Act. These courts entail the risk of irreversible miscarriage of justice with no recourse to appeal for the accused, a point that brings into question their legal veracity. There is only fragile support for the Military Courts and a number of religious groups are directly opposed to it. Reading between the lines it can be seen that the democratically elected civilian Government is now incapable of coping with the internal security issues that envelope the nation, especially the dissonance that comes with religious extremism, and has turned to the Army for assistance. The Army has used this situation to entrench its position in the body politic of the nation as an indispensable protector of its sovereignty.

The NAP is supposed to usher in a policy of 'enlightened moderation'; and recognises the need to regulate the madrasas if the virulent tide of Islamic radicalisation that is sweeping the country is to be controlled and eventually reversed. However, other than the Military Courts that have started to function, the NAP so far seems to be a paper exercise. A lack of political will to follow through with the lofty ideals set out in the Plan is transparently visible. Further, with the ISI itself radicalised to a great extent the NAP is unlikely to bear any tangible result, irrespective of the intentions of the Army.

Currently there is a visible lack of support for liberal activists, who are being targeted at will across the country by the religious extremist elements, the right-wingers. Already embroiled in the Tribal region, the Army is unwilling and perhaps also lacks the capacity to effectively interference in this deteriorating situation. Lip service is all that is available at the moment to the liberal activists. In the latest disturbing development, the IS has made deep inroads in Karachi and some other parts of the nation. They exploit the historical fault lines of the Sunni-Shia rift and stock anti-Shia sentiment to which the State has so far closed its eyes. The anti-Shia sentiment seems to be legitimised by the Sunni Ulama religious organisation that has been State-backed since the 1950s.

Sectarian demagoguery is increasing in the entire nation. In Karachi, the Federal Government has initiated a drive against gangsters and terrorists, since 5 September 2013. The partial success of this drive has had unfortunate consequences in that it has provided increased space for the more radical Islamist fanatics to operate. Pakistan today is dominated by unconstrained religious extremism and the arrival of the IS into the mix increases the threat of sectarian violence exponentially. The politico-army arrangement provides only a tiny shimmer of hope in this darkness. Another fall-out of the military lead in securing the country is that the situation definitely diminishes the strength of civilian institutions, which can have long-term detrimental effects to Pakistan evolving into a truly democratic State. It looks as if the wheel is coming full circle in Pakistan with the relevance of democracy being covertly questioned. The only difference this time is that the Army is content to play the puppet master rather than perform on the centre stage.

Looking at the manner in which the elected Government and the Army is going about trying to secure the nation, it seems that Pakistan does not understand the need to institute radical change—it is still pursuing reckless policies without any thought for the security of the nation, and is being driven purely by religious ideologies and compulsions that have become entrenched in its body politic.

Pakistan – Afghanistan's Challenge

Afghanistan and Pakistan have historical misunderstandings at the strategic level and continue to nurture them. The new National Unity Government in

Afghanistan, led by President Ashraf Ghani, has made overtures to Pakistan to create a conducive atmosphere to usher in peace. An agreement on intelligence sharing has been signed between the ISI and its Afghan counterpart National Directorate of Security (NDS) with the aim of making Pakistan alter its policy towards Afghanistan. This is a simplistic approach from an inexperienced Afghan Government and has already cost the President political support at home. However, there is no getting away from the fact that Pakistan is critical to peace in Afghanistan, since the Taliban is dependent on Pakistan's support to continue their insurgency. Pakistan's Afghan policy is purely Army controlled. There is also a viewpoint that over a period of time the Taliban have gradually become more independent, especially after the withdrawal of NATO forces, and therefore, the influence that Pakistan has over their activities is in decline and exaggerated; although this change in the equation is something that cannot be categorically verified.

Almost immediately after signing the agreements, the Afghan President criticised Pakistan for not doing enough to reign in the Taliban who have refused to come to the negotiating table. In all this flurry of activity, of accusations and counter-accusations, a long term vision for peace in Afghanistan is not discernible. The activities are all at the tactical level and the political process that is critical to further peace initiatives at the strategic level cannot be detected. At the moment, the Taliban continue to move across the Durand Line, the de facto border between the two countries, at will in either direction with no effort visible from Pakistan to stop this cross-border incursions. Even China, Pakistan's all-weather friend, has not been able to persuade it to take effective steps to stop cross border terrorist activities. In this confusing game of decision and indecision, the IS has been making steady inroads into the region.

As in most cases of terrorist activities emanating from its soil, Pakistan has maintained a completely different narrative regarding the Taliban in Afghanistan. Afghanistan had expected Pakistan to ensure that the Taliban would not start their customary 'Spring Offensive' this year, but Pakistan has not obliged. The Afghan-Pakistan relationship is fragile, to put it mildly. The distrust continues and last week Afghan lawmakers accused Pakistan of providing refuge to Taliban leaders on their side of the border. In turn Pakistan has resorted to its age old strategy of declaring that it has nothing to do with the Taliban and washing its hands off the entire issue. In comparison, the original 'washer of hands' Pontius Pilate, would have been put to shame.

Underlying this charade is the fact that Pakistan considers Afghanistan as a contested territory with India, mainly for influence. After the September 11 attacks on the World Trade Centre, Pakistan was acutely aware of the need to keep on the right side of the United States, and accordingly resorted to double-dealing. On the one hand they train, promote and export terror and extremists, while also giving the impression of fighting them. Under these circumstances Pakistan is unlikely to force the Taliban into peace talks. The question however remains—do they have that kind of influence on the Taliban anymore? The double-dealing seems to have so far achieved its purpose, since the US continues to pump in aid to the country, while it continues to train and export terrorists.

The India Factor

Pakistan invariably accuses India for any mishap that takes place inside their country. The proverbial foreign hand is always blamed. So it is no surprise that Pakistan accuses the R&AW, of fomenting trouble in Baluchistan and the tribal areas, although no convincing evidence has been produced. Anti-India propaganda has been an on-going norm in Pakistan for decades and clever media strategies have increased the magnification of the allegations. The Army increases the pitch of the rhetoric whenever there is a need to muddy the waters when it becomes necessary to distract and mislead the domestic public opinion or to thwart foreign policy initiatives from India that is perceived as being against the interests of Pakistan. The recent case of the Army propaganda machine going into overdrive during the Indian Prime Minister's official visit to China is an illustrative example. The move was meant to scuttle any rapprochement between India and China. An anti-India stance has always been, and continues to be, the one single focus of Pakistan in all aspects of its national interest.

The Blind US and All-seeing Pakistan

The US strategy—if it can be called a strategy—in its dealings with Pakistan has always been based on what the US wants to believe rather than on ground realities. The US wants to believe that Pakistan is trying to defeat and neutralise the Taliban, while in actuality the Taliban could not have withstood the onslaught of the US and its allies and continued as a fighting force without the active support of Pakistan. In Afghanistan the US is fighting the Taliban, who is being supported by Pakistan, who is a US-ally. What is going on here?

There is a long history of US appeasement of Pakistan, while Pakistan has been consistently undermining US interests in the region. Viewed dispassionately, it is not difficult to see that Pakistan is not a 'problematic' ally, but a cynical and manipulative nation serving its own purpose and nothing else. The fundamental flaw has been that in 2001 the US believed that Pakistan indeed wanted to be a responsible partner in the 'war against terror'. In this blind belief, the US reimbursed Pakistan for its contribution to the war and set up the Coalition Support Fund (CSF) to pay for putative Pakistani support for NATO troops in Afghanistan. The CSF has already disbursed around $13 billion to Pakistan. A 2008 US Government Accounting Office report was scathing about Pakistan cheating regarding the accounts of the fund. However, the funds have not been abolished and continues to be used to 'bribe' the country to ensure that the Pakistan Army continues to stay and fight the insurgents in the Federally Administered Tribal Area (FATA). Who has ever heard of a nation getting paid by an external government to protect its sovereignty and integrity?

The fact is that Pakistan has been using the US supplied funds to buy arms that are meant to fight a conventional war with India and not an internal counter-insurgency conflict, and the US has turned a blind eye towards this misuse of international funds, provided in good faith. Since the World Trade Centre attacks in 2001 and Pakistan enthusiastically joining the war on terror, the US has transferred a large number of military equipment to Pakistan: One Perry-class frigate; 18 new and four used, nuclear-capable F-16 fighter aircraft; 500 air-to-air missiles; 1,450 2000-pound bombs; 1,600 kits to convert unguided bombs to laser-guided munitions; 2,007 anti-armour missiles; 100 Harpoon anti-ship missiles; seven naval guns; 374 armoured personnel carriers; and 15 uninhabited aerial vehicles. It would seem that the insurgents that the Pakistan Army is fighting in the remote tribal regions have developed extraordinarily potent air, naval and ground force capabilities! At least by US reckoning.

Pakistan has over the years carefully cultivated the perception within the US policy-making establishment that it is 'too important to be allowed to fail'—built on the often mentioned possibility of nuclear weapons falling into the hands of terrorists, if Pakistan disintegrates as a State. This is playing on the inherent fear in some Western capitals. Further, Pakistan wages a selective war on terrorism, dividing the terrorists into 'good' and 'bad': the good ones being the groups that follow Pakistan's instructions and export terrorism into neighbouring countries, principally India and Afghanistan; and the bad ones being the groups that create mayhem within Pakistan itself. It is easy to deduce that the principle tool of foreign policy for Pakistan now is terrorism.

Conclusion

It is time that the international community started to treat Pakistan as what it is—the breeding ground of terrorism. The US has to read the writing on the wall—however blind it may have become in the past 15 years. Accommodation and appeasement has run its course, with disastrous results both for US and its allies, as well as for Pakistan. It is time for the US to initiate a massive overhaul of policy and hold Pakistan to account not only for the enormous amount of wealth that has been poured into the nation, but also for its nefarious activities that have led to death of thousands of US and NATO troops. This policy has to be fully rooted in sober realism and an understanding as well as acceptance that it was US-supplied funds that were directly used to resource the current Pakistani terrorist and nuclear capabilities. Any other course of action will be an affront to the free-thinking people of the world. Pakistan, the land of the pure, is playing a catastrophic game of deceit and is not so pure and innocent as it likes everybody to believe. Even in diplomacy there are certain times when a spade must be called a spade.

Published in Eurasia Review 22 June 2015

http://www.eurasiareview.com/22062015-pakistan-stuck-in-a-cul-de-sac-analysis?utm_source=feedburner&utm_medium=email&utm_campaign=Feed%3A+eurasiareview%2FVsnE+%28Eurasia+Review%29

6

SAUDI ARABIA

CHARTING A COMPLEX COURSE

From the very beginning of their rule of the Saudi kingdom, the al-Saud family has embraced the principles and practices of the Wahabi ideology, an extreme and strict version of Islam. The support for the extreme variety of Wahabi teachings increased in 1979 after Ayatollah Khomeini came to power in neighbouring Iran, the primary supporter of Shia Islam. In a bid to counter the spread of Iranian influence in the region, Saudi Arabia orchestrated the formation of the Gulf Cooperation Council (GCC) that was embraced by all the Arab monarchies. However, Wahabism has been supported and used also by the Western powers—primarily the US and UK—in three distinct initiatives, to support their own interests. First, early in the 20th century, both the US and UK supported the spread of the Wahabi ideology to wean the Arabs away from Turkish Ottoman influence, which practised a much more tolerant and open interpretation of Islam. Second, in the 1950s, Wahabism was used by the US to curb the rise of Arab nationalism led by Egypt's President Nasser. Third, in the 1980s the US used Wahabism to oppose the Soviet occupation of Afghanistan, in the process indirectly radicalising the Arab youth in the Middle-East.

The combined result of the Saudi Arabian and Western support of Wahabism, to meet their own narrow and short term goals, has been that two or even three generations of Middle-Eastern youth have grown up subscribing to a religious belief that has set aside the qualities of mercy, compassion and benevolence advocated throughout the Holy Quran. This rigid and extremely violent interpretation of the practice of the Islamic faith is the fundamental issue that throws up myriad other challenges in the Middle-

East and now impacts the entire international community. It is through this lens that the actions of Saudi Arabia in the past few months must be viewed.

Saudi Arabia today faces three major challenges to its well-being: the increasing regional influence of Iran; the Islamic State (IS) making inroads into the kingdom; and a vexed relationship with the US. Of the three issues, the rise of Iran and the manifestations of its spreading influence are considered the most immediate threat to the regional leadership ambitions of Saudi Arabia. When the implications of a powerful Iran are analysed from a Saudi viewpoint, the compulsion for their direct intervention in the civil war in Yemen becomes easier to understand.

Background to the Intervention in Yemen

It is purely Saudi Arabian aid that has kept Yemen afloat for decades. The Saudis have supported the military, security apparatus, education, social services, and transportation projects—in short almost all government services are partially or fully Saudi funded, which has prevented Yemen from becoming a failed state. The Saudi aim, unlike what some sceptics believe, has not been ideological influence but a pragmatic attempt to ensure stability in Yemen to avoid state failure and thereby ensure the stability of the southern region of Saudi Arabia. The south-western Saudi Arabia was separated from Yemen and annexed by the Saudis in the 1930s and the tribes of the region are ethnically Yemeni. In terms of national security that part of Saudi Arabia is therefore the most vulnerable. The tribes in southern Saudi Arabia have not converted to Wahabi Islam and the fear in Riyadh is that they could either join with the Houthi uprising in Yemen and/or start a domestic rebellion.

Further, Saudi Arabia has for years accused Iran, rightly or wrongly, of interference in the domestic politics of Yemen and of backing the Houthi rebels. However, Iran's influence over the Houthis is tenuous at best, although they benefit from the largess of Tehran in providing much needed arms and other resources to continue the civil war. It is not sure that the Houthis can be ordered about by Iran to fit in with a larger Iranian plan to become a Middle-East hegemon.

The Saudi-Iran rivalry goes back to the overthrow of the Shah by the Ayatollah and the establishment of a decidedly Shia theocracy. The Saudis have always supported Sunni extremism, and Iran has reinforced Shia movements. It is unfortunate for Saudi Arabia that their initiatives have backfired spectacularly, to an extent wherein their on prodigies are now threatening Saudi national security. In recent times, Iran has provided unconditional support to Iraq for the fight against the rise of the IS whereas Saudi response has been hamstrung, for a number of domestic reasons. This has led to an increase in the regional influence of Iran and resulted in the perception of a change in the balance of power in favour of Iran. This is anathema to the Saudi ruling family who claim and believe that they are the unquestioned leaders of the Middle-East.

In this situation, if Saudi Arabia wanted to retain the Arab leadership role, there was no option but to start a process to diminish Iranian influence. Theoretically being on the same side in the fight against the IS in Iraq, the military intervention in Yemen therefore became unavoidable. It was relatively easy to put together a coalition consisting of the GCC members to increase the legitimacy of the intervention, although at the initiation of the military campaign the UN Resolution had remained short of permitting military action. The subsequent UN Security Council Resolution 2216 of April 2015 demands that the Houthis retreat from all Yemeni cities that they have captured and lay down their arms to facilitate the return from exile of the 'legitimate' government back to Yemen. The Saudi-led coalition insists on this as a precondition for stopping the air campaign. They also want the international community to enforce the resolution, citing the 1991 expulsion of Iraq from Kuwait as an example, and also stating the Resolution 2216 provides the best chance to arrive at a long term solution to the Yemen imbroglio. However, realistically it has to be accepted that in this instance international military intervention will not take place.

The Coalition

The Saudi Arabian monarchy did not have any difficulty in convincing the Arab League, GCC countries and both the US and Turkey to join the coalition once the decision to intervene in Yemen had been made. It is not the composition of the coalition, but the nations that are not part of it that is indicative of the fault lines that have developed in the Arab world, and perhaps more importantly, in the overarching society of Islamic nations. Egypt was vociferous in its support in the beginning, even suggesting the possibility of a ground invasion, but of late has been opaque in its official statements regarding a ground assault into Yemen. However, if Saudi Arabia decides to take that route, it is highly likely that Egypt will be coerced to be part of the invading force, even if reluctantly. The fiasco of their earlier intervention in Yemen is not completely lost in the Egyptian military memory.

Turkey has also been all noise and very little substance in their support for the intervention. At the start of the air campaign the official stance was revealed in careful statements that said the government may 'carefully consider' providing 'logistic support' based on the progress of the situation. Turkey's attitude to the intervention is political pragmatism at its best. Initially Ankara demanded that 'Iran and terrorist groups' withdraw from Yemen; an understandable rhetoric considering that it needs Saudi Arabian assistance to tide over its current economic trouble. Turkey's current public debt is the highest it has been in a decade. However, it also knows that Yemen is a tough nut to crack, especially without the use of ground forces, and that Saudi Arabia is in a bit of a quandary. On Iran's strong reaction to its comments, Turkey hurriedly back-pedalled, putting out a call for an end to the war and recommending the quest for a 'political solution', a very different tune to what had been played few weeks earlier.

The support from the Arab League has been varied with a majority being on-side. However Iraq opposes the intervention and Algeria has called for an end to 'all foreign intervention' in Yemen. The GCC is a placid and compliant organisation that normally toes the Saudi line. In this case, Oman with a shared border with Yemen has voiced concerns regarding the intervention, obviously because of worry regarding the possibility of a spill over of the chaos into its own territory.

Pakistan is the other Saudi ally that is conspicuously absent from the coalition, both in terms of military participation and also in rhetorical statements of support. The Yemen intervention is not popular with the public in Pakistan and the Parliamentary decision to stay away from the campaign reflects this. However, the decision has made the once-solid Saudi-Pakistan relationship wear thin. The Saudi Arabian support for the extremist elements functioning within Pakistan has turned public opinion against the kingdom, even though they have been Pakistan's benefactors for decades.

The role of the US in the coalition is easy to describe but difficult to understand in terms of identifying the objectives that it hopes to achieve. The US position is uncomfortable, having taken sides in what is essentially a civil war by providing arms, logistics, and detailed intelligence and targeting support to the coalition. This stance is completely opposed to the current administration's stated policy of keeping out of 'turf' wars. Even Saudi Arabia's close allies Pakistan and Turkey have refused to be drawn into the conflict, fully understanding the difficulties in taking sides in an all-Islamic fight. In directly assisting Saudi Arabia, the US will in all likelihood create another sectarian adversary in the Houthis and possibly Iran. Although it is worried about the increasing influence of AQAP, and aware that they are not being targeted by the coalition, the US has opened arms transfer facilities to Saudi Arabia. It is apparent, from statements and interviews of senior US military and government officials, that the US does not have a clear visibility or understanding of Saudi Arabian strategic goals behind the intervention. The coercive use of air power in an all-out bombing campaign to achieve political solution to a convoluted problem has almost no chance of success. However, the US lacks the political will, and perhaps does not have the diplomatic edge anymore, to pressure Saudi Arabia to agree to a ceasefire.

Saudi Arabia has always relied on its financial power to be the centre piece of its diplomatic initiatives. This approach does not seem to be working in the current circumstances. With the progress of the nuclear negotiations with Iran, there is a high likelihood of sanctions against the country being lifted. When that happens all nations, including the GCC countries and Turkey, will want to ensure their share of the gold rush which will inevitably follow. Cash for loyalty has always had a short term life cycle.

The Air Campaign

Considering that after more than two months of air strikes in Yemen, which has grown increasingly controversial in terms of the targeting of civilian infrastructure, the Houthis still control large parts of the country and the 'legitimate' government is still in exile in Saudi Arabia, the inevitable question has to be asked, 'Was the intervention a strategic mistake?' There is no doubt that the intervention was popular among the Saudi population in the initial phase, although the support seems to have become ambivalent as the campaign has dragged on. The air campaign has very little to show, other than the destruction of the limited infrastructure of an already poor country and the killing of around 2000 civilians in a rough estimate.

This is not the first time that air power is being used in Yemen to quell a rebellion. In earlier days both Britain and Egypt had used air power extensively in separate attempts to put down rebellions and failed miserably in the attempt. There were two common reasons for these failures. One was the mountainous terrain that provided the rebels with impervious natural cover from aerial attacks and the other, the glaring eye of the international media that negated unbridled use of firepower from the air, ensuring that the air forces consciously minimised collateral damage. The current Saudi air campaign is also affected by the same constraints and could well follow the failed imperial initiatives of the 1960s.

Although the air campaign is continuing, it seems that whatever could be achieved has been achieved, which points to the fact that a ground campaign may be necessary to return President Abd Rabbo Mansour Hadi and his government from exile to Sana'a as the legitimate ruler. Saudi Arabia has been training Yemeni fighters to mount a ground campaign to drive out the Houthis. However, tangible progress in this initiative will require a long lead-time and even then the chances of success are limited. Saudi Arabia will not commit its own ground forces to an invasion in what promises to become an absolute quagmire. It is increasingly apparent that the only way forward is a negotiated political settlement. Any such settlement will only hold true with the participation of Iran and the current climate of Saudi-Iranian regional rivalry precludes their arriving at an amicable settlement. In effect the air campaign has so far only created a humanitarian disaster in which the common people of Yemen are bearing the brunt of the privations.

The initial objective of the air campaign was to obtain air superiority over Yemen by degrading and neutralising the minimal air power capabilities of the Houthis, which consisted of a few MiG-29s armed with Kh-29 and Kh-31 guided missiles. This was achieved in the initial phases of the campaign and some Scud missile facilities that escaped were subsequently destroyed. The second objective was to achieve control of the strategic Bab al-Mandeb straits in the south-west coast of Yemen, which is the fourth busiest shipping bottle-neck in the world. This was also achieved through a combination of naval blockade and air action. The Saudi strategy is based on the belief that control of the seas and the air is sufficient to contain any threat to the kingdom.

The rebels control much of the territory in Yemen and it will take a protracted, large-scale ground invasion to drive them back to their initial positions in the north. Can air strikes alter the balance of power on the ground in this scenario? An honest answer would be that it is unlikely under the current circumstances. The containment strategy therefore is obviously meant to create the necessary conditions for negotiations. The current situation and the inability of the air campaign to create any further progress brings out few questions.

Was the intervention meant to be a demonstration of strength for the consumption of the domestic population of Saudi Arabia? Was there a miscalculation in terms of the military support expected from the allies?

There is no doubt that the strategic aim of the intervention was to curtail and push back a burgeoning Iranian sphere of influence. However, it also provided an opportunity to demonstrate the ability of the new ruling elite— both king and his inexperienced aides—to initiate decisive action in order to stabilise their power-base within the large al-Saud family. An easy victory would have achieved that purpose admirably. It can also be surmised that the possibility of a ground invasion would have been envisaged with the assistance of both Pakistan and Turkey. The fact that the Saudi planners did not even consider a refusal from these two 'old' friends is evident in the way in which the broad campaign has played out. In both Pakistan and Turkey real politick triumphed over decades-old alliances. Iran is a major and powerful neighbour to both these nations and they cannot afford to antagonise an emerging power.

The Situation inside Yemen – The AQAP Gains

To put it succinctly, the situation in Yemen is such that absolute confusion reigns. The initial swift advance of the Houthi militia has run out of steam. They are now short of fuel, food and water and are reverting to a holding pattern, although their actions do not seem to be oriented towards consolidating their gains. They are now being opposed by rival factions in the south and central regions of the country. However, these factions are not united under one banner and also despise the President in exile, Mansour Hadi, as much as they despise the Houthis. Since they are fragmented they have not been able to gather the momentum or the power necessary to push the Houthis back into the northern mountains. In the meantime some of these factions have started to form unsavoury alliances with the Al Qaeda in the Arabian Peninsula (AQAP), which has always been a deadly fighting force.

In a generic manner there are two demons to fight in Yemen—the sectarianism that was not very obvious even a few years back, and regionalism that has been the bane of the country for decades. Even today, separatist movements in the South have not given up their demand for an independent country, 25 years after the unification in 1990. It can be argued that a bit more than two decades is a very short span of time for independence movements to be fully subdued, and therefore the separatist movement is to be expected.

The US has been mounting a UAV campaign against AQAP form few bases in Yemen for a number of years, which was one of the major factors in the AQAP being unable to gain any distinct advantage in their operations in the Arabian Peninsula. At the advance of the Houthi forces, the US contingent had to vacate the country, thereby giving the AQAP a much-needed respite. Paradoxically, the Saudi Arabian air campaign has had the unintended consequence of the AQAP being able to gather fresh momentum for their activities. Within a very short time, they have expanded the territory under their control and there is a visible improvement in their strength and a dramatic increase in their activities. The US support to the Saudi air campaign that has benefitted an adversary that they have been trying to contain for a number of years itself presents a dichotomy at the strategic level.

The increased presence and operations of the AQAP is not being countered or targeted by the Saudi-led coalition air strikes. The air campaign is focused on ensuring that Iranian assistance to the Houthi fighters is fully and completely severed. In the meantime AQAP is going from strength to strength. Again a sort of short-sightedness is visible in this military strategy. The AQAP has declared, at its inception almost a decade ago, that they consider Saudi Arabia the immediate enemy and believes that the monarchy lacks the legitimacy to rule the kingdom. The AQAP is more a threat to Saudi Arabia than to any other nation and yet the air campaign is not even tangentially targeting them. Strange is perhaps a very weak term to describe this bizarre military strategy.

The air campaign has not managed to curb the power of the Houthi militia. In 2009 Saudi Arabia had intervened in Yemen with troops on the ground to fight the same tribal caucus. The attempt failed then and the rebels could not be defeated; it is even more unlikely that the Houthis will collapse this time around if a ground invasion is attempted. Saudi Arabian military planners are very aware of the pitfalls of embarking on a ground offensive.

There are few imponderables that emerge from this confused situation. First, it is easy to believe that Iran is only involved to an extent that is necessary to ensure their own security, although the means of achieving it through support to Houthi militia is a questionable strategy. Even so, considering the strong Saudi support to Sunni-led extremism across the Middle-East, Iran's support to minority Shia sections is perhaps understandable in an extreme sort of manner. However, if the currently on-going nuclear negotiations were to fail, Iran's reaction to the Saudi intervention in Yemen cannot be predicted. Second, the war in Yemen is obviously aimed at winning back the cities, territories and ultimately the loyalty of the tribes, superimposed by the ever present sectarian twist. The Saudi-led coalition seems to be content for the time being with creating and ensuring a state of chaos and instability with an increase in the sectarian divide in Yemen. So far Yemen has not been divided on sectarian grounds and the air campaign is slowly driving a wedge into the sectarian homogeneity of the State. The only winner in both these cases is the AQAP.

Into the Future...

It is unclear as to who is actually winning the war. The air campaign in its current guise is ineffective and counter-productive to the promotion of a political solution. It has proved to be a poorly thought-out military adventure by the newly installed Saudi king and his inexperienced son, who is today the youngest Defence Minister in the world. It has brought about unfathomable human misery to the poorest region in the Arabian Peninsula. On the other hand, Yemen cannot conceive of a bright future without ensuring good relations with Saudi Arabia. Iranian military support to the Houthi militia will continue although an outright rebel victory is highly unlikely. The civil war has all the hallmarks of becoming a festering wound. Further, Iran will not be able to replace Saudi Arabia as the major benefactor of Yemen to create stability. In the current stand-off situation, a stable and prosperous Yemen remains a faraway chimera.

Even when analysed from all angles, a Saudi exit strategy, other than with the complete withdrawal of Houthi forces, is not visible. It is possible that this entire situation has been created by the hubris of a new and unproven Saudi leadership that wanted to exhibit political and military dominance of the region. The continuing air campaign is a manifestation of its failure and the insertion of ground troops, if that happens, will be further indication of strategic failure.

It is clear that both sides want and hope for a negotiated settlement. However all political diplomatic avenues that could lead to a ceasefire and settlement requires the participation of Iran and obviously of the Houthis themselves. Even so, only a political solution can bring this sad episode to an end. If Saudi Arabia perseveres with their insistence on severing the Iranian connection and the complete withdrawal of Houthi forces, the deadlock is also likely to continue. Any continuation of the air campaign will create a failed state and the only winner will be the AQAP. The need of the hour is the rise of a statesman of vision and calibre who can not only bring the warring factions to the negotiating table and hammer out a peace deal, but also ensure that the factions honour the deal. It seems a far-fetched dream.

Published in Eurasia Review 10 July 2015

http://www.eurasiareview.com/10072015-saudi-arabia-charting-a-complex-course-analysis?utm_source=feedburner&utm_medium=email&utm_campaign =Feed %3A+eurasiareview %2FVs nE+%28Eurasia+Review%29

7

TURKEY ENTERS THE MAELSTROM

Turkey is a NATO member and its location at the confluence of Europe, the Middle-East, the Caucasus and the Balkans is a definitive strategic advantage. This location and its history have provided Turkey with ethnic, religious, linguistic and cultural connections with a large number of nations, some of which may not even share a geographical border with it. However, the same factors can also become a restraint to the actions that the nation can initiate to ensure its security. Modern Turkey is cognisant of its identity and conscious of its current pursuit of an evolutionary ideology while being wary of its slightly troubled relationship with NATO. The overarching strategic concept of NATO is still understood in the Turkish higher level decision-making, but in the past four years the divergence of interests regarding the approach to regional security between the two has become visibly apparent.

The same period has seen the intensification of the Civil War in Syria and the forceful emergence of the Islamic State (IS) on Turkey's borders. In dealing with these two challenges, there is a clear discrepancy between the primary objective of the US and that of Turkey—the US wants to defeat the IS before attempting to remove Syrian President Bashar al-Assad from power, whereas Turkey considers his removal the fundamental objective to be achieved. Turkey has so far not been able to alter US focus in any appreciable manner. In a show of pique, Turkey had reacted by boosting cooperation with the natural rivals of NATO and the West. While the Western nations were imposing sanctions and resorting to military bellicosity against Russia over the events in Ukraine, Turkey expanded its economic and political cooperation with Moscow—increasing the Turkey-Russian trade to $ 100 billion a year. It also signed an agreement to build a $ 20 billion nuclear power plant with

Russian collaboration. The icing on the cake in these initiatives was the signing of a $ 4 billion deal with China to procure long-range missile systems.

President Recep Tayyip Erdogan had led the nation into a new paradigm where the possibility of a strategic break in relations with the West was no longer anathema to national security. Instead, the new Turkey would create its own traditions of co-existence with both the West and the East, generating national power by once again becoming the bridge between the two. The traditional strength derived from close relations with NATO became overshadowed by the altered perception of national identity, closely aligned to a more Islamic version of the State. The ruling Justice and Development Party (AKP) is ideologically aligned with the banned Muslim Brotherhood of Egypt and blames the Western nations for the current chaos in the Middle-East. The AKP came to power 13 years back in what was decidedly a secular nation but ever since has single-mindedly pursued an agenda of gradual Islamisation.

The AKP's Islamic Agenda

It is true that a minimal amount of Islamisation had started in the 1950s with the establishment of a parallel Imam Hatip Secondary School system aimed at producing theologians. Erdogan is himself an early product of this system. In 1980, the Islamic character of Turkey was endorsed in the constitution. Since its inception, the AKP has viewed Turkish secularism as a historical travesty and on coming to power accelerated the Islamisation process. This initiative is manifest in the changes that have been made to the education system, in keeping with Erdogan's repeated mention of the need to 'raise a pious generation'.

The AKP government has changed the curricula from Kindergarten onwards, doubling the number of Imam Hatip schools from 453 to 952 in one decade with the enrolment going from 90,000 to 474,000 between 2004 and 2014. In 2014, the Higher education Council made non-Islamic studies in Universities such as courses in the sociology of religion, and philosophy optional while Islamic sciences like Koranic exigencies remain compulsory. The State's goal is to gradually demolish Western-inspired teachings and return Turkish education to an Ottoman-inspired 'greatness'. There is a palpable sense of the AKP embracing symbolic gestures to further the Islamisation of the nation.

The issue is that the Islamisation process is slanted towards a Sunni interpretation of the religion, whereas Turkey is home to a large number of minority sects. For example, there are over 10 million Alevis, who follows the traditions of Shia'ism imbibed with Sufi influence and has affinity towards the Alawaite sect of Syria. The Syrian refugees, majority of whom are Sunnis, have moved into the Alevaite heartland and in combination with the IS controlling large segments of the border, has created increasing tensions there. The AKP needs to establish a visible balance between religion and the existing plurality of the State to stabilise the situation.

And then came the national elections on 7 June, the results of which upset the AKP's applecart.

The Elections and its Immediate Aftermath

The AKP and its autocratic leader President Erdogan were confident that they would once again win more than the 367 seats needed to have absolute majority in parliament. It was perceived that thereafter the constitution would be amended to make Erdogan the Executive President of the country with absolute power, akin to a dictator. However, the people of Turkey spoke through the ballot box—for the first time since coming to power in 2002, the AKP won only 258 seats, and less than 50 per cent of the votes, reaching a figure of only 41 per cent. The pro-Kurdish People's Democratic Party (HDP) won 80 seats and 13 per cent of the votes, more than the mandatory 10 per cent required under electoral laws to cross the threshold and be represented in parliament. The vote was a clear mandate for pluralism and an indicator that the people wanted to move away from Erdogan's increasingly autocratic and Islamised rule. This election has produced the most inclusive Parliament in Turkish history and is a clear call for maintaining diversity.

There are a number of reasons for the decline of the AKP's electoral mandate. The immediate reason was the Islamist-influenced populism that Erdogan and other leaders of the AKP had been practising for a number of years. Their high-handed approach to popular demands has made over half the country to side with other parties in an election that had a voter turnout of 86 per cent. Over a period of time the AKP had criminalised dissent through passing anti-blasphemy laws and sweeping anti-terrorism bills. The Turkish people were aghast at the Government's widespread suppression of dissent, the lack of respect for the rule of law, and the political opportunism displayed in whitewashing economic corruption. In their hubris, the AKP had forgotten the lessons of history; the Turkish people had always baulked at top-down social engineering, and the rejection of the grandiose dreams of the AKP in the June election should not be considered a surprise.

Other factors that contributed to the AKP failure are also equally important. First, the AKP was quick to support the Arab Spring-related civil strife in neighbouring countries and almost became the de facto leader of the uprisings. This attitude created rifts between Turkey and some of the more powerful Arab monarchies. Second, the Turkish Government reversed its friendship with President Bashar al-Assad and started to support the rebels wanting to oust him from power. To achieve this purpose, it kept its borders with Iraq and Syria open as a conduit for deluded international recruits to join the IS. Further, Turkey did not permit its indigenous Kurdish population to assist the besieged Kurdish town of Kobane located at its border with Syria. Since the beginning of the international coalition's military operation against the IS, Turkey has considered Syria to be the bigger threat to its security and has considered the Islamist groups fighting there as some sort of allies.

The Kurdish Issue

The AKP had explored all possible avenues to make sure that the HDP did not cross the mandatory 10 per cent of votes in the elections, even having the HDP attacked in 60 of the 81 provinces by proxy, as was reported. The HDP is opposed to Erdogan personally and promotes a democratic future for Turkey. Therefore, the AKP knows that the HDP will not permit the creation of a presidential system of government, which seems to be Erdogan's ultimate personal aim. The HDP is also indirectly affiliated to the banned Kurdish Workers Party (PKK) which has led an insurgency in Turkey for three decades. Before the Battle of Kobane, there was a faction of Kurdish religious people who were pro-AKP. But after the Turkish Government refused to assist the Kurdish defenders of Kobane they shifted allegiance; the fact is that Erdogan wanted Kobane to fall to the IS in order to diminish the Turkish Kurds' influence in the country.

Turkey has been watching with growing unease the close cooperation between the Syrian Kurdish militia, known as the Peoples Protection Units (YPG), which is the armed wing of the Democratic Union Party (PYD) that is affiliated to the PKK. The AKP has been debating the options available to curtail the Kurds' ambition to have an independent State. By end-June, the YPG had become the most important ally of the US in the fight against the

IS. YPG had direct communication links to call in US air strikes as required and US assets were also providing ISR to them. With increasing Western collaboration the Kurds routed the IS from Tal Abyad, a strategic town on the border with Turkey. The Kurdish battlefield successes further strained their relationship with the Turkish leadership. Further, the tenuous peace between the Kurds and the Turkish Government that had held for nearly two years ended with the Kurdish electoral success. Turkey's biggest fear now is that the creation of a Kurdish homeland, even with limited autonomy, will subsume parts of its own territories in Anatolia. Therefore the AKP views Kurdish autonomy anywhere in the Middle-East as a greater threat to its security than even the IS.

In Turkey there is now a clear and visible demarcation of Turkish and Kurdish nationalism. The Kurdish gains in Syria has added further impetus to Erdogan's government to try and stem the rise of Kurdish identity and their demand for independence. Turkey's long-standing demand to establish a 'buffer zone' in northern Syria is a direct response to the perceived threat from the Kurds. For long the US had not been in favour of creating such a zone, but they had not catered for the opportunistic manipulations of the AKP. Till mid-July the US had steadfastly maintained that only the tangible defeat of the IS by the Syrian Kurds, with the assistance of coalition air strikes, would let it attempt a regime change in Syria. In these circumstances Turkey had mentioned the concept of creating a 'buffer zone' unilaterally, but this was more rhetoric than an actual plan of action. An attempt to achieve a buffer-zone would have involved heavy fighting with both the IS and the Kurds, something that the Turkish military did not want. Military intervention in the Syrian Civil War did not have majority public support in Turkey. Then came the suicide bombing in the Turkish border town of Suruc on 20 July that killed 30 Turkish citizens and injured over 100, creating a political opportunity for the AKP to get what it had always been clamouring for—dismantling the gains the Kurds had so far made towards their independence.

The adverse election result was a catalyst for the government to initiate action against the PKK members and persons linked to IS through internal crackdowns that also saw the interdiction of IS supply lines. This put in motion the cycle of IS sponsored suicide bombing, Turkey's retaliation through strikes against IS and PKK camps, and the PKK's increased insurgent violence in Turkey. It is possible that the PKK sponsored violence in Turkey could result in a reduction in the votes that the HDP had garnered earlier, when a re-election is ordered, providing a window of opportunity for the AKP to gain majority and continue its agenda of constitutional amendment.

Turkey in the Line of Fire

The Middle-East is in the throes of a serious, multi-cornered and violent power struggle. Turkey, while debating the use of military force to ensure its interests are not trampled on by the violence just across its borders had exercised restraint so far—the cost of failure of military intervention was far too high in the current confused circumstances. It was also cognisant of the political chaos engulfing the region and the difficulty in dealing militarily with amorphous insurgent organisations. Turkey therefore had adopted a policy of avoiding direct involvement in the on-going Middle-East imbroglio while also retaining the maximum number of options open. This meant not cooperating with the international coalition battling the IS. Turkey had elected to follow a diffused strategy that did not need any committed decisions to be made to deal with the growing challenge in the neighbourhood. It is very similar to the broad US strategy in the region, but the Turks seemed to have forgotten their geographical proximity to the threat.

An election reversal and a terrorist attack at a critical moment in the AKP's political manoeuvring changed the entire complexion of Turkey's Middle-East policy. The attack on Suruc by the IS brought the US and Turkish intentions regarding the way forward somewhat closer than it has ever been before. In very quick order Turkey arrived at a quid pro quo understanding with the US: Turkey would permit the coalition air forces to operate from its Incirlik air base in return for the creation and maintenance of a buffer zone 100 kilometres long and 40 kilometres deep, west of the River Euphrates. The agreement would enable a step-change in the US air campaign while Turkey would at last realise the buffer zone—a de facto IS-free 'safe-zone'— that it had clamoured and demanded be set up from the beginning of the Syrian Civil War. On 23 July Turkey launched its first air strikes of the campaign against the IS and also attacked PKK militant camps in Iraq, after having sat on the sidelines for almost a year.

It has been reported that the Turkish Air Force send in 75 F-16s and F-4Es in three waves between 24-26 July dropping 300 smart bombs in 185 sorties that attacked approximately 400 PKK targets. Turkey has indeed shifted from a hands-off approach to one based on emphatic use of military power.

Ankara has made yet another complete U-turn and become fully committed to the US-led air campaign. From a US-perspective a new strategy seems to be emerging. If the northern IS-free zone can also be duplicated in the south of Syria, then it may be possible to contain the IS between the two corridors and after whittling them down through air strikes, eliminate them with ground operations conducted by a combination of the Free Syrian Army, the PYD militia and even Assad's own forces, with the Western coalition providing air strikes.

The Challenges and Dichotomies

The AKP in Turkey—which still lacks a mandate to form the government—was quick to equate the IS and the PKK, a move that the US either chose to ignore or was blindsided by the swiftness and ferocity of the Turkish air attacks on the PKK. At least for now the Kurdish fighters, rather than the IS, seem to be the primary target of Turkish air strikes. By bombing the Kurds Turkey hopes to gain the strategic upper hand against the PKK and also prevent the PYD forces from encroaching into Turkish territory. Simultaneously Turkey has arrested more than 600 IS militants and conducted operations against PKK's urban infrastructure within the country. The main reason for this level of frenetic activity is that Erdogan hopes to leverage the nationalistic feeling that comes with going to war to cobble a malleable coalition to further his own and the AKP's future political agenda. Viewed in a cynical manner it seems that since the June elections derailed Erdogan's bid to become the uncontested supreme leader of Turkey, he has taken the country to war in the hope that wartime frenzy would make people give the AKP a majority in a snap election that can be called in November. There just may be some truth in this assessment.

At the moment the ground realities are this: the US military is turning a blind eye to the Turks targeting of the same Kurdish militia whose close coordination with US air power was critical to pushing back the IS from Kobane and curtailing their ability to manoeuvre, while the Turkish forces sat on the sidelines, willing the IS to win. The US seems to be enamoured by the concessions that Erdogan has placed in front of them, while the hard fought battles and victories that the Kurds brought them in the past year seems to have gone out of their collective memory. There is a trap being set here, because from all the events that have taken place so far it seems that Erdogan has only one mission—to ensure that the AKP has an effective majority in parliament so that he can then change the constitution and become the executive President of the country. If democratic principles are trodden over in this process, so be it, after all the ends justify the means.

From the time that Turkey has started air strikes, the only visible trend is that their fundamental objective is to rein in the Kurds. The US-led coalition has assisted the Kurdish YPG militia to fight the IS and they have been by far the most effective combatants on the ground. The fear of an independent Kurdish state being created along Syria's northern border with Turkey fills the AKP leadership with absolute dread and it is clear that they will do anything to ensure that such a situation is not realised. Therefore, Turkey is in the process of establishing a 'buffer zone' in north-west Syria which will also be a buffer against Kurdish nationalist aspirations. Whether or not the US approves this thrust seems at least for the present to be of no consequence.

What the world has to accept, however hard it may be, is that Turkey has over the past decade been gradually turned into a police state. It was easy for the government to arrest and detain 'suspects' who are either sympathisers of the IS and also PKK members or supporters. The AKP government has cleverly used the one suicide attack in Suruc to effectively rebalance the electoral gains the Kurdish HDP had made. Erdogan is finding alternative methods to claim his coveted goal of becoming the ruling President.

Conclusion

There is a fundamental dichotomy in the aims of the 'new' partners—US and Turkey. The US wants the IS defeated conclusively before a regime change is orchestrated in Syria, for fear of the IS filling the void rapidly if Assad is removed before that. Turkey is single-mindedly pursuing the ouster of Assad and the defeat of the Kurdish militia as the highest priority. Further, the two countries do not agree on a common definition of the 'buffer or safe zone' that is being created in Northern Syria. In an indirect manner the US-Iran nuclear deal also swayed Turkey's calculations. It was felt that the Iranian deal would lessen Turkey's influence with the US and therefore the offer of the use of the airbases in Turkey was meant as a direct inducement to bring US back into a position favouring Turkey.

Turkey is not overly concerned about the caliphate dreams and designs of the IS, they know that other (read Western) powers will contain it. Turkey's fundamental objective is driven by their hatred for Kurdish ambitions and now they find themselves in the happy position of the US supporting them, if not overtly then at least turning a Nelson's eye to the direct action being initiated against the Kurds. If ever there was a people caught between Scylla and Charybdis, it is the Kurds. Other minorities in the region must watch, learn and understand how quickly a global power can turn its back on them, even before their usefulness to the grand scheme of things is fully exhausted. The current turn of events make a mockery of friendships and alliances, of loyalty and fidelity, of steadfastness to the achievement of an objective through morally correct action. One sees the triumph of opportunism and the demonstrated ability of a great power to once again turn away from its smaller and vulnerable allies. Cynical self-centredness is perhaps too soft a term to describe the current attitude of the two new-found allies.

Published in *Eurasia Review* 10 August 2015

http://www.eurasiareview.com/10082015-turkey-enters-the-maelstrom-analysis/

8

THE IMPROBABILITY OF PEACE IN SYRIA

The regime of President Bashar al-Assad now effectively controls only about one-sixth of the territory of original Syria and its control is diminishing on a daily basis because it is losing territory to insurgents and facing a manpower shortage in the military. Till recently the regime continued to hold the core urban centres across the country while letting the countryside, mostly desert, be controlled by the opposition groups including the Islamic State (IS). On 26 July, Assad admitted that the regime had difficulty in holding on to all the provincial centres that it had so far endeavoured to do and that it would now concentrate available military resources on securing the Damascus-Homs-Hama-Latakia coastal belt in the west. The IS is attempting to move into the regions that have been abandoned by the regime. The undeniable fact is that Syria has already been dismembered into several 'fiefdoms'.

The Syrian Civil War has now been raging for four years and there does not seem to be any end in sight. The major participants are the Assad regime and its primary supporters Iran and Hezbollah, the IS, Turkey, the moderate Southern Front, the Saudi Arabia sponsored Islamic fundamentalist group Jaysh-al-Fatah and the al Qaeda affiliate Jabhat-al-Nusra. In addition the Kurds are extremely active as are the Western nations fighting an air war against the IS. Somehow, if these groups could be aligned into two distinct camps it may have been easy to understand the civil war. Unfortunately each one of these entities have different and self-serving objectives and, perhaps more importantly, are at odds with each other.

The Assad regime is essentially fighting three main enemies—the IS, which holds almost half of Syrian territory although much of it is desert; the Islamic rebel coalition Jaysh-al-Fatah that is supported by Saudi Arabia, Turkey and Qatar; and the Southern Front, a moderate opposition coalition that holds much of the south of Syria. The regime is supported by Hezbollah and both have suffered heavy personnel losses to an extent that they can no longer carry on a three-sided conflict. They seem to have therefore decided to let the IS fight the other Islamic groups and the moderate opposition. Assad's calculation in doing so is not difficult to fathom—if and when the IS is able to defeat the other groups, the international community will come to his aid to fight the scourge of IS. This sequence of events can only be considered a pipedream, fundamentally because of the fact that if IS remains the only opposition to the regime, the international forces are unlikely to fight to keep Assad in power. The only reason he is allowed to continue to hold on to some vestige of power is because the international community does not want the IS to fill the vacuum that would be left in the wake of the removal of Assad. Therefore the current tactics of letting the IS fight the others is bound to fail in the long term.

The Southern Front

The only remaining moderate opposition to the regime is the Southern Front, which openly renounces extremism. From a military perspective this group is relatively well organised and has support from the US and some European countries. The Front controls the provincial centre Daraa about 100 kilometres from Damascus. The changed tactics of the regime has facilitated the IS to take on the Southern Front, indicated by the situation on the ground where from early 2015 almost all the battles that the Southern Front has fought have been against the IS—the regime and Hezbollah are not engaged anymore.

The Southern Front is now the only moderate group that can stand up to Jaysh-al-Fatah and other more fundamentalist groups. To its credit, it has provided ethical guidelines for its members and has also established a political wing in preparation for an anticipated political role in the inevitable transition that has to take place in Syria. The Front works closely with the local civilian councils in the areas that it controls and has managed to gain the trust of the citizens, much more than any other group. This has resulted in people joining the group not out of ideological support, but in order to ensure social order and stability in today's extremely turbulent time. Further, the Southern Front hopes to wean members of the less fundamentalist groups to join them, although this might require greater financial capabilities since other groups, especially the Jaysh-al-Fatah provide financial incentive to its members. The Front needs greater financial and military assistance if it is to prevail against the better supported groups.

Saudi Arabia and Jaysh-al-Fatah

Since the beginning of the war against IS, Saudi Arabia has felt that the flagging of its regional influence. The situation was exacerbated by the US-Iran deal that led to the international community's acceptance of the Shiite nation and Iran's increasing influence in the region. Saudi Arabia expects that removing the Syrian President, who is supported by Iran, from power would bolster its position and lead to greater regional influence. The Islamic group Jaysh-al-Fatah was created by Saudi Arabia as a pragmatic response to the US ambivalence regarding a regime change in Syria, which from a Saudi Arabian viewpoint is critical to improving their influence and to achieve any further progress in resolving the conflict.

Even in the creation of one more fundamentalist organisation, Saudi Arabia is playing its usual double-game. It supports the Southern Front against the regime in Southern Syria while actively involved in supporting the Jaysh-al-Fatah in the north and also trying to create a branch to function against the Southern Front in the regions under its control. Riyadh also wants Jaysh to be independent of Jabhat-al-Nusra, the Syrian franchise of al Qaeda. This requirement is being emphasised since currently there is some amount of affiliation between the two groups. Only with complete delinking of the two can Saudi Arabia and Qatar hope to have predominant influence in the post-Assad Syria. If the Jaysh-al-Fatah manages to outgrow the Southern front, it will become the most influential militia inside Syria and will play a significant role in Syria after Assad is removed, a situation that will effectively sideline all other moderate groups.

Jabhat-al-Nusra, the al Qaeda affiliate is sensibly moderate in its approach to the conflict, but also harbours political ambitions. However, the group has also made it clear that its objectives are restricted to being an influential element within Syria and that it does not entertain any global ambitions. Its fundamental political objective is to influence Syria's transition and to ensure that it becomes an 'Islamic' nation.

The Turkish Factor—Kurds and IS

From the beginning of the US involvement in the Syrian Civil War the US has concentrated on defeating the IS, while Turkey, Saudi Arabia and Qatar have focused on ousting Bashar al-Assad. While the US has supported the Kurds as 'effective partners' on the ground in the fight against IS, Turkey and the others supported opposition militia in their fight against the Assad regime. However, there is no unified command amongst these militia to achieve the removal of Assad and there is no consensus regarding the shape of the post-Assad Syria. Ankara is the joker in the pack, with President Erdogan steadfastly insisting on Turkish hegemony over a transitioned Syria. Turkey perceives Syria and the Kurds as the fundamental threats to its security. The US disagrees with this assessment but have not been able to convince Turkey that defeating the IS is critical for any other regional initiative to succeed. Till such times as Turkey joined the military alliance against Syria and started taking part in the military operations, it was banking on the Islamic groups who were sympathetic towards Turkey and operating in Syria to remove Assad from power.

Although the Kurdish militia has been the most effective fighters against IS on the ground, Erdogan has reopened the Turkish civil war with the Kurds instead of attempting to achieve a negotiated settlement for a more durable peace. Currently the official chatter in Turkey is about the 'Kurdish threat' to national security, encouraged by the AKP government to achieve its declared aim of preventing the formation of an independent Kurdistan. The AKP government is pursuing the perpetuation of dual tactics. One, to create a 'buffer zone' in northern Syria so that the land area controlled by the Syrian Kurds will not be contiguous to set up an autonomous Kurdish state; and two, rounding up Kurdish activists within Turkey to prevent them from initiating any action towards a 'greater' independent Kurdistan.

Turkey finally entered the war last month (July 2015), after four years of siting on the sidelines and cheering the wrong teams. It faces two direct threats along its southern border—the IS and the Kurds. The IS controls large swaths of desert between Aleppo in north-west Syria, Mosul in northern Iraq and Ramadi in the south near Baghdad. Turkey denies abetting the rise of the IS, although they maintained a porous border from 2012 to 2014 and turned a Nelson's eye to the influx of large numbers of weapons and foreign fighters crossing it to join the IS. This was obviously done in the mistaken belief that the IS would have an easy victory over the Assad regime. They did not cater for the tenacity of the Syrian government and the support it would receive form Iran and the Hezbollah. Turkey also stoked the anti-government resentment of the Sunnis in Iraq by repeatedly accusing the al-Maliki government of having a Shia bias. Turkey has consciously attempted to destabilise Iraq through increased support for IS in Iraq and more importantly through its support for Kurdish autonomy in northern Iraq. Turkey continued to aid both the Kurds and IS by buying oil from them, over al-Maliki's protests. The Frankenstein is now coming home to roost.

Turkey had undertaken a brutal repression of domestic Kurds in the 1980s and 90s, who still account for about 20 per cent of the population. It is also noteworthy that the Kurdish rate of population growth is higher than the national average and therefore this percentage is likely to increase into the future. Apart from Turkey, the Kurds are spread over Syria, Iraq and Iran with their fight for independence starting to gain traction with the arrival of IS into the fray. Currently the Kurdish controlled areas of Iraq and Syria can be considered almost a single entity. Turkey has realised that the Iraqi-Syrian Kurds are now far advanced in their quest to be an autonomous State and are fearful of the influence it will have on their own Kurdish population. Tukey fears that it may not be able to stop Turkish Kurds from joining their brethren. If this happens, it would translate to the loss of about a quarter of Turkish territory where Kurds are in majority. Such a turn of events, would see Turkey losing its common borders with both Iraq and Iran and suffering a commensurate decrease in its regional influence.

This is where the Turkish demand for the 'buffer zone' comes into play. It is significant that the creation of a 'buffer zone' has been Turkey's fundamental demand from the beginning of the Syrian Civil War and denial of which was primary reason for Turkey so far not joining the fight. Turkey has a two-fold aim in the creation of this zone, nominally north of Aleppo in areas currently controlled by IS—one, push the IS away from its southern borders while filling up this 'safe zone' with Syrian refugees; and two, by doing so they will prevent the Kurds from linking the eastern and western parts of the territories that they control. Logically such a buffer zone should be controlled by the Kurds since it lies in Syria and is essentially a part of the Kurdish territory but Turkey will not let them take control. In combination with the domestic crackdown on Turkish Kurds, this situation could lead to a sub-conflict in the region.

Turkey has also calculated that if the 'buffer zone' is established then the Jabhat-al-Nusra will be able to concentrate fully against the Assad regime, because the IS will not be able to attack it from its flanks. This is a secondary bonus in Turkish calculations since their primary aim remains the removal of the current Syrian regime from power. Turkey is essentially superimposing its domestic political compulsions on the Syrian Civil War. This is Erdogan's risky gamble, since it can benefit Turkey only to a point—the Kurdish issue cannot be swept under the carpet nor can an ostrich-like attitude lead the way to peace and stability. Return to the negotiating table with the Kurds can only happen after the train of events that Erdogan has set in motion runs its course and much blood—both Turkish and Kurdish—is spilt on the streets and sand of Turkey.

Iran's Peace Initiative

The Iranian foreign minister, Mohammad Javad Zarif, has put forward an updated version of an earlier peace proposal, which has a four-point agenda: cessation of hostilities within Syria; a five-year transition period; retention of Syrian sovereignty; and the expulsion of all foreign terrorists from Syrian territory. Unlike the last time, this proposal is likely to be debated seriously by the major parties involved because of two factors—Iran's greatly improved status and re-entry into mainstream international politics following the 'nuclear deal'; and the extensive consultation that was done with Qatar, Kuwait, Lebanon and the Syrian regime itself before the plan was announced in public. The plan is for extensive political dialogue to be conducted among the Syrian people when physical combat ends in order to chart an acceptable way forward.

The problem with the Zarif Plan is; first, the difficulty in enforcing the cessation of fighting considering the wildly different hues of the parties involved, second getting Turkey on board, and third, creating a transitional Syrian Government acceptable to all. The need, as everyone recognises, is to arrive at a negotiated settlement. The longer the conflict lasts, greater are the chances of the IS increasing its influence in failing Syria. Even Russia, so far a staunch supporter of Assad, recognises that Syria could rapidly become IS country and therefore it is common sense to unite against the IS. The transitional government, if it ever gets established, needs to have representation across the Syrian political spectrum and should include the opposition diaspora as well as members of the current regime willing to shift their stance. It has to be a compromise solution and must avoid all the challenges that Iraq faced when a less than optimum solution was foisted upon the people after the 2003 invasion.

The antagonism inherent in the Turkey-Kurd relationship complicates the implementation of the Zarif Plan. The Plan also discounts the fact that the IS will not negotiate with any of the other groups or countries involved and must therefore be defeated in order for the peace process to proceed. Turkey holds the key at the moment to the way forward. However, at least for the moment it seems that unless the Kurdish issue is sorted out Ankara will continue the impromptu responses that it has so far put forward without any consideration of the long-term strategic consequences of such actions. At the absolute baseline the chances of establishing successful peace comes down to Turkey-Iran relations. While their bilateral relations remain satisfactory and trade is gradually being boosted, the interventionist policy that Turkey is currently following may in the end become a bone of contention. The gravity of the situation in Syria requires secondary and self-centred interests to be set aside. The real threat remains the fact that the Syrian could rapidly engulf the neighbouring countries.

Conclusion

The Syrian conflict has not only dismembered the nation but has ravaged the greater Middle-East. While there has been continuous air strikes by the US-led coalition against the IS, no grand strategy has been articulated or is being followed. Containment as a strategy is an open admission of a dearth of imagination. Neither has any political agreement followed in the footsteps of all the diplomatic activity that has been carried out with more than adequate fanfare. The challenge now is that the civil war is not a Syrian Civil War anymore, it is a Middle-Eastern Civil War in which the opponents are not clearly divided, where friends become foes and foes become allies in very short order, creating a confusing mosaic of half-truths and grey areas. There are far too many parochial interests being pushed and a number of proxy wars being fought in Syria, leading to the reluctant conclusion that a considered political solution recognised by all participants can never be achieved.

No one nation, group or alliance has the strength or quantum of force necessary to regain control over the lost territories in Syria in order to stitch together even a fractured State with geographic credibility. The US and its allies do not have a coherent strategy to bring about an acceptable solution so that the people of Syria can start to rebuild their ravaged lives. It seems inevitable that Syria will continue its path towards complete fragmentation. The threat of IS is real, but the complete dismemberment of Syria will have far greater consequences than what the IS currently pose in the region. Meanwhile as the world watches and waits—more than half the Syrian people have become refugees in their own country; their erstwhile ruler continues to bomb his own people; and the IS destroys millennia old artefacts in the name of religion. Syria's death knell is audible, loudly and clearly.

The nations of the Middle-East and Turkey should be carefully listening the sounds and remembering the words of the 17th century poet John Donne, 'Any man's death diminishes me, because I am involved in Mankind; And therefore never send to know for whom the bell tolls; It tolls for thee.'

Published in Eurasia Review 25 August 2015

http://www.eurasiareview.com/25082015-the-improbability-of-peace-in-syria-analysis/

9

AFGHANISTAN: FRAGILE AND FORGOTTEN

Deliberate and repeated insurgent attacks, endemic corruption within the governing polity, a shrinking 'formal' economy, the end of a development boom as a more than decade long international war draws to a close that in turn has created unemployment levels of 35 to 40 per cent and a deteriorating security situation has the year-old Government scrambling to keep Afghanistan afloat. Proxy wars and external powers' political manoeuvring are returning to the country—history is repeating itself. Historically Afghanistan has always been at the mercy of the great powers of the day, its geographic position making it strategically critical as a tool to be used to extend the influence and interests of one 'Empire' against the other. Afghanistan was the buffer zone in the 'The Great Game', the rivalry between the British and Russian Empires in the 19th and early 20th centuries, and more recently in the aftermath of the Soviet occupation in the 1980s, the country has become the political battleground of regional and international power play.

A Foreign Policy Vacuum

Afghanistan was recognised as a state on 19 August 1919 and has ever since been aligned to one or the other great power to ensure its stability. Accordingly, its foreign policy has always remained ambiguous in an effort to be aligned with the benefactor of the time. However the current Government, under President Ashraf Ghani and CEO Abdullah Abdullah, realises that the future of Afghanistan is intimately intertwined with its foreign policy and that its alignment with other powers determines the stability of the nation.

Foreign policy of a nation is enshrined through smart diplomacy focused on ensuring national interests. Political scientists argue and agree that small and fragile states need not have a declared foreign policy since they do not have the economic, political or military means to pursue and ensure their policy interests. It is believed that foreign policy of such nations will always be shaped by external forces, and will mostly be beyond their control. It is indeed true that in the prevailing international system, fragile states have no control over their future. While not always being fragile, Afghanistan has had very little control of its foreign policy because of the geopolitical games played by other nations. In the 18th and 19th centuries the sparring between British India and Tsarist Russia was played out in Afghanistan and after World War II, the Cold War imperatives impacted on all foreign policy issues of the nation. After the fall of the Taliban regime in 2001 and more than a decade of conflict later, today Afghanistan continues to be in the unenviable position of having no clear policy direction and suffering from a long-term policy vacuum. The situation is exacerbated by the lack of consensus within the Afghan political elite regarding the direction that would lead the country to stability.

As and when a tangible foreign policy is crafted it will have to take into account the fundamental factors of the prevailing geopolitical situation and the national economy. It is within this context that President Ghani's foreign policy initiative to stabilise the nation must be analysed.

The Geopolitical Situation

Afghanistan is riddled with geopolitical challenges and has become a safe haven for al Qaeda and other global jihadist groups, the latest in this list being the Islamic State (IS), which is clearly trying to establish a foothold. The lack of strategic direction and purpose that the Government has displayed and their inability to implement Government decisions for the past decade has made it impossible to prosecute these groups effectively. This weakness in governance has been a boon for regional militants who have set up camp in Afghanistan. The probability of cross-border terrorism into its territory has made Pakistan feel threatened, especially when it is undertaking a military campaign in their tribal areas that share a common border with Afghanistan. China is also increasingly worried about the support that their Uighur insurgency could receive from the transnational terrorist groups settling into Afghanistan.

On coming to power, President Ghani made a concerted attempt to improve relations with Pakistan, whom he views as being critical to ensuring stability. In doing so he went against the common belief in Afghanistan that Pakistan was fundamentally responsible for the terrorist activities that destabilised the country. The Afghan Taliban operates out of the safe havens in Pakistan where they are supported by the military intelligence arm of the Pakistan Army, the ISI. Even as the President was making his overtures to Pakistan, the Taliban carried out a series of back-to-back suicide bombings in August this year and followed up by perpetuating a number of attacks in Afghanistan. Ghani has directly blamed Pakistan for these attacks and asked that the Taliban safe havens in Pakistan be closed down. In this confused scenario, the IS has made gradual inroads with the intention of weaning disgruntled Taliban and al Qaeda operatives to its flag.

For South and Central Asia the importance of Afghanistan is based on two factors—it has substantial and as yet unexplored mineral reserves and it straddles the energy transit route between the two parts of Asia. China particularly is concerned with the continuing violence that threatens the viability of their growing investment in Central Asia and its efforts at expanding its footprint in the Afghan mineral sector.

The National Economy

The Afghan economy is fully dependent on foreign aid and military contracts. However, this was always not the case. Prior to the country descending into the current crisis, its economy was based on tourism, and the export of lapis lazuli, dried fruits, and carpets. Subsistence farming was also practiced although the country has never been self-sufficient in food. The growth rate now is only 1.5 per cent and from an economic perspective the country is a failed state with a dismal image. However, Afghanistan has vast quantities of natural resources and minerals that can be extracted to make the nation economically viable. Optimal exploitation of these resources would require technical and financial capital, which is currently unavailable to the government. Any initiative to revive the economy must have a long-term plan that in turn requires an enormous amount of political will, institutional capacity for implementation and overarching and sound policy directives backed by foreign investment on a gigantic scale. Sadly, none of these ingredients to success are currently on display in Afghanistan.

Transitory Peace Talks and Mullah Omar's Death Announcement

In early July, the Afghan Taliban had been coerced into attending peace talks held in Murree, Pakistan, which was orchestrated and sponsored by the US, China and Pakistan although one faction of the Taliban which runs the Qatar political office boycotted the meeting. However, the revelation, after the first round of talks, of Mullah Omar's death in Karachi more than two years ago negated the possibility of further negotiations. In any case, the only agreement that was reached in the first round of talks was the intent to meet again. Since the announcement of Mullah Omar's death on 29 July, the Taliban has backed away from the promised second round of peace talks. The entire peace process is now 'on hold', with no visible future schedule.

The manner and timing of the announcement of Mullah Omar's death makes one pause to analyse the motives behind it. The initial news was given out by a splinter Taliban faction of limited influence known as Fidai Mahaj and was almost immediately confirmed by both the Afghan Government and the US. It is interesting that Pakistan did not deny it, while not also confirming it. Mullah Omar while he was alive was demonstrably averse to any negotiations with the 'un-Islamic' democratically elected government. The Taliban cadre had vested some sort of a mystic divinity around the personae of Mullah Omar and stood united purely on the strength of this belief. Since Mullah Omar was notoriously reclusive and the entire cadre was actually being run by his Deputy Mullah Akhtar Mansoor, it suited Pakistan to keep his death secret, to further entrench Mansoor's hold over the group.

There has always been a strong and enduring relationship between Mullah Mansoor and the ISI who was instrumental in installing him as the Deputy. Mansoor headed the Quetta Shura and has for long operated out of Pakistan's Baluchistan Province with the full support of the ISI. It is also reported that he was educated in a madrasa (an Islamic seminary) in Jalozi village located in Naushera district of the Khyber Pakhtunkhwa province of Pakistan. His loyalty to the ISI runs very deep. However, Mansoor had only a very tenuous control over the Qatar faction who stayed within the fold only because of their reverential attitude towards Mullah Omar.

The revelation of Mullah Omar's death, full two years after the event in a Karachi hospital at this juncture, can therefore be considered to be an ISI sponsored act of necessity to ensure Pakistan's strategic stake in Afghanistan.

Since early 2015, Pakistan has been informing the international community that it is willing to give up its interest in Afghanistan if the Taliban were to be accommodated in the emerging power structure of the country. If this was to be achieved, then Pakistan would become the custodians of the peace in Afghanistan and the puppet masters of the Taliban under Mansoor. However, it seems that something went wrong in this calculation and therefore the ISI now wants to sideline the Taliban factions that are inimical to its interests so that it can institute Pakistan's own policy goals in Afghanistan.

Mullah Omar's death is shrouded in mystery and there are rumours already floating that he was poisoned. The Taliban cadre have started to question the motive and the authority behind keeping his death secret for so long. The death announcement has definitely accentuated long standing schisms within the Taliban and effectively closed the chances of a negotiated settlement in Afghanistan. It also opens the doors to leadership challenges since Mullah Omar was the only unifying factor within the group. Almost immediately on the announcement of his death rifts became visible in the Taliban. Mullah Mansoor, supported by the ISI, claims the leadership but is not universally accepted as the leader. The brother of Mullah Omar, Mullah Abdul Manan and his son Muhammad Yaqoob maintain that the successor should be from the same clan. The tensions regarding the succession have reached a point wherein the Taliban political chief in Qatar, Tayyeb Agha, has resigned.

Pakistan's Duplicity

In this emerging imbroglio, it is difficult to fathom Pakistan's game plan and intentions. Pakistan is under pressure from the US to check the Taliban activities in Afghanistan and China also has indicated that it would not want a Taliban takeover in the country. Pakistan is also realising that with the announcement of the death of Mullah Omar, their overarching control over the Taliban is reduced. Their control over Mullah Mansoor now does not translate to influence over the entire Taliban, which was supposed deliver strategic control of Afghanistan to ensure stability—the one carrot that was being offered to the Ghani Government.

Mullah Mansoor is not accepted by all the factions of Taliban and lacks legitimacy to enforce his will. There are indications that the rifts—both tribal and ideological—that had so far been papered over by loyalty to Mullah Omar, have come out as open divisions. That this situation will derail any meaningful progress in the peace process is a foregone conclusion. The current situation provides a window of opportunity for the Afghan Government to create an opening to stabilise the nation, although it may be something of a gamble.

At the moment Mullah Mansoor cannot sell the peace process to all Taliban factions, especially the radical groupings. The gamble would be for the Government to push Mansoor, with Pakistan's assistance, into a peace deal although such a process will undoubtedly split the Taliban with the high possibility of the splinter groups joining the IS. This scenario could perhaps not be counted as a success and in any case is dependent on the willingness of Pakistan to pressure Mullah Mansoor to come to the negotiating table. Pakistan's efforts at the moment will be focused on ensuring that the Afghan Taliban remains a single entity since a split will further destabilise the security situation within Pakistan where the domestic Taliban have started to pledge support to the IS. Therefore, the future of the peace talks is fully dependent on Mullah Mansoor's ability to persuade the entire Afghan Taliban to accept him as the single supreme leader, which is highly unlikely to happen. At this juncture in Afghanistan it would seem that even the chance of arriving at a settlement with one half of the Taliban is a gamble worth taking.

Pakistan is currently in a bind. The strategy of proxy wars and negotiations that it had orchestrated is unravelling rapidly. At the same time the Afghan Government in Kabul is asking them to step up the pressure on the Taliban to stop the terror bombings and restart the peace talks. However, Pakistan's control over the Taliban is now not that strong, especially when factional struggles are on-going. Further, the Qatar faction of Taliban is critical to the future of Afghanistan, but is anti-Pakistan. It is possible that this faction is being supported by the Middle-Eastern Gulf powers and being developed as an antidote to Pakistan's overwhelming influence, with the tacit approval of the Afghan Government. It is obvious that Pakistan underestimated the challenge of controlling Afghanistan through proxies and pursued a misconceived approach to achieving it. The ultimate paradox in this complex performance is the Afghan Government seeking Pakistan's 'co-operation' to deal with the terrorist activities of the Taliban that have been unleashed by Pakistan itself.

There is no indication that Pakistan in trying to reign in its terrorist proxies or attempting to abandon its quest for strategic control of Afghanistan. On the other hand there is mounting evidence of Pakistan's deceitful attitude towards all negotiations with Afghanistan. It continues to use terrorism as the primary instrument of state policy to destabilise all its neighbours. However, the joker in the pack is the IS and its claims to a Caliphate that is slowly taking root domestically and which is likely to change the game in Pakistan. Pakistan is playing with fire, with not a care to its own safety.

Afghanistan – Fledgling Steps to Nationhood

Afghanistan today is in a state of exasperation, staring at an uncertain security situation and an unpredictable future. Its domestic imperatives always trump foreign policy requirements and its internal stability is intertwined with its relations with regional powers—not an ideal formula for stability. The National Unity Government (NUG) has been in power for almost a year and the nation still harbours cautious optimism based on an understanding that after decades of conflict and confusion the path towards peace is long and progress normally slow. The NUG is an uneasy power sharing arrangement, primarily between President Ghani and the CEO Abdullah Abdullah, made necessary in order to assuage the two major ethnic communities in the country—the Pashtuns and the Tajiks. The Hazaras form the third major group, although there are 14 ethnic groups in the country, each supported by a different regional nation.

Afghanistan has been ruled by the Pashtuns for the past two centuries and therefore they are averse to change, even in terms of alterations to their accustomed lifestyle. The Tajiks and the Hazaras are better educated and have always formed the administrative and bureaucratic backbone of the nation. Their greater literacy makes them amenable to change and adoption of moderate approaches to social and cultural issues. However, they have very limited understanding or experience of wielding power. Although sectarian conflict is very rare in Afghanistan, the inherent diversity of ethnicity, language, and culture directly and adversely impacts the cohesive development of a national consciousness that could surpasses narrow parochialism.

The Government is focused on furthering the peace process; and so it should be. However, the diarchy of power sharing and dual control of the government machinery are not conducive to smooth functioning, especially when such an arrangement often leads to mundane personality issues overriding other more serious considerations. Further, there are rifts within the Government with the National Security Directorate (NSD) considering the Taliban a terrorist organisation, while the President is attempting to negotiate with them. The NSD does not want a power sharing arrangement with the Taliban, who in turn aspires to return to power in the country that they ruled before being ousted in 2001 by the NATO-led coalition. The Taliban have a long term vision and appropriate strategies in place to achieve this objective.

In Afghanistan there was scepticism regarding President Ghani's peace initiative with Pakistan, which has turned into active questioning of Pakistan's credibility in furthering the process after the recent wave of terrorist bombings attributed to its proxies. It is reliably reported that about 4100 Afghan soldiers and police have been killed and almost double that number injured in the first six months of this year, a 50 per cent increase in comparison to the same period last year. It seems that the ISI is pursuing its own agenda, playing a different game keeping Pakistan's own domestic agenda as the highest priority, with the Pakistan Government unable to control it. That too is nothing new, the ISI has been a law unto itself for several years now. The possibility of a split in the Taliban could make the ISI change its tactics, but the policy of employing terrorism as a strategic weapon will not change.

India, the other regional player in the game, is visibly concerned with President Ghani's attempt at reorientating Afghan foreign policy through negotiations with the Taliban under the aegis of Pakistan and China. It feels sidelined, especially after it has played an important role in funding and assisting in reconstruction efforts towards infrastructural, educational and capacity-building projects in Afghanistan. There are strong cultural links between India and Afghanistan and Afghanistan government has openly acknowledged India's assistance in providing higher education facilities to its people. However, the current initiative does not include India, which is perturbed by its being kept out of the core dealings in the peace process.

There are some facts that must be stated before a broad solution to the challenge of Afghanistan can be contemplated. First, Kabul by itself will not be able to contain the Taliban, even in its splintered form. Second, co-opting the Taliban for peace talks is not conducive to progress since they are part of the problem and cannot be an integral part of the possible solution. Third, the Pakistan Army wants strategic control of Afghanistan and therefore continues to foster the Taliban as a major factor in the stability calculus—a retrograde step in the long-term stability equation. Fourth, a preponderance of evidence is now available to clearly label Pakistan as a force that is bent on destabilising the greater South Asian region who should be kept out of any involvement in the Afghan peace process.

The US military withdrawal weakens the Afghan Government's position in negotiations and the recent ISI sponsored terrorist attacks undermine its credibility with regard to providing basic security for its citizens. From Afghanistan's perspective, the nation is on a route of enduring troubles leading to a complex and tortuous future. However, a strategy to create stability based on pragmatism and reality is unfortunately nowhere in sight. International support to the embattled nation is now critical to achieving tangible progress in stabilising the volatile situation. Even a semi-permanent solution to Afghanistan's deepening woes can only be achieved with international and regional participation, committed to keeping Afghan interests at the highest priority without bias. If an enduring peace leading to long-term stability is not achieved through sustainable reconciliation, the Afghan challenge will embroil the entire South Asia in a tumultuous turmoil. The future, at least in this devastated part of the world, is predictable.

Published in Eurasia Review 8 September 2015

http://www.eurasiareview.com/08092015-afghanistan-fragile-and-forgotten-analysis/

10

THE ISLAMIC STATE

UNDERSTANDING AND COUNTERING ITS STRAGEY

The Islamic State (IS) has been fighting the combined military might of the US-led coalition for over a year without having been contained or defeated as was promised by world leaders at the start of the war. The term 'war' is being used after due consideration, for what is going on in the Middle-East cannot be explained as anything else. The IS has emerged in one year as the top global jihadist movement and dominates the international security scene. Its attraction to new recruits and believers alike has been the physical creation of a State, which has been declared the new Caliphate that does not recognise geographical borders.

There is a prevailing belief that the IS is the product of the ill-conceived invasion of Iraq by the United States (US) and its allies in 2003. This is only partially true—the invasion was merely the catalyst that coalesced an enduring tension. The group is more the product of the gradual encroachment of religious fundamentalism into Arab politics that has progressively weakened the social, cultural, moral and political conditions of the Middle-East and North Africa, permitting hardened religious ideology to superimpose itself over the morass. The struggle that IS champions, while being part of the sectarian and ethnic conflict raging across the region, is more a battle to create a recognisable societal identity rather than being part of power politics.

Background

The current prominence of the IS can be traced back to the narrative shaped by al Qaeda that was aimed at creating an Islamic powerbase that could face up to and counter the perceived, and at times actual, Western hegemony in international affairs. This was further embellished by sowing the seeds to encourage the belief of the West being the enemy and a direct threat to the wellbeing of Islam as an entity. The proverbial clash of civilisations was cleverly converted into religious antagonism and blamed squarely on the Western world. The apparent defeat of al Qaeda facilitated the IS in positioning itself as the logical successor to the weakened group. It created the necessary military and political framework to move forward, with the initiative being supported by the severe disaffection and frustration of the Sunni population in Iraq. It is noteworthy that each new manifestation of political Islam is more virulently fundamentalist and extreme than the previous iteration that it replaces.

The IS now possesses a highly trained and flexible military arm and controls sufficient resources to stave off attacks by a large, multinational coalition created for the sole purpose of defeating it. The fundamental difference between the IS and al Qaeda, existing as a shell of its former powerful entity, is the IS's explicit and declared desire to create a Caliphate. Towards this end it displays centralised control at the strategic level that increases and focuses its effectiveness. There has been two significant consequences of the arrival of the IS on the scene. One, the concept of secularism has completely disappeared from the Middle-East. Two, the Islamic world has been engulfed by a rebellious religious turmoil created by the exacerbation of the basic schism between the Sunni and Shi'a sects, which is difficult if not impossible to pacify. The IS has leveraged this situation by institutionalising religious ideology and further wedging the existing sectarian rupture. It directly targets the ideas and reconciliatory concepts that have kept Middle-Eastern religious extremism under check for many decades. The only redeeming factor, at least for the moment, is that the IS is still contained within the territory that it has so far captured.

The Coalition

Any coalition is only as good or as bad as the sum of its parts. The US-led coalition that is currently fighting the IS in the Middle-East consists of a number of partners who are at odds with each other and openly pursue their own individual objectives, irrespective of the coalition priorities. The Middle-Eastern members particularly have domestic political imperatives that influence their actions on the battlefield. Some of them have continued to provide covert support to their 'favourite' radical groups operating in the region with their own agendas. Saudi Arabia's position is a classic example. It is one of the major coalition members but its strategic view is clouded by Iran-phobia and the perceived necessity to be seen as the champion of Sunni Islam, not only in the region but also globally. In accordance with this belief, Saudi Arabia equates the Iran-supported Houthis of Yemen as equally damaging to regional stability as the IS. The reality is nowhere near this perception.

Turkey, a relatively new member of the coalition, considers the IS as a controllable entity that has to be harnessed to enhance its own regional powerbase. Turkey's domestic imbroglio with the Kurds and the fact that the IS is virulently anti-Kurds makes this assumption more palatable. It also continues to emphasise that Bashar al Assad is more of a threat than the IS. Within this farce of a coalition, the US and its Western allies are trying to bottle up and isolate the IS within a designated geographic area so that it can then be deliberately targeted and destroyed. However, such an operation can only succeed if the nations with shared borders with the IS territory collaborate fully and are committed to the laid down objective. This is not the case at the moment.

The Gulf nations have created a Saudi-led coalition of their own to defeat the Houthis in Yemen, fundamentally based on prosecuting an air campaign. This air power coalition could perhaps be made the mainstay of the campaign against the IS, if and when the Western nations decide to leave. From a purely military perspective this is feasible, but the countries lack the political will to focus on defeating the IS. The friction between the members is openly visible and is indicative of the major issues that trouble the region— the distribution of power that is not accepted by all and is therefore dynamic; an inherent distrust of other nations, based on ethnicity and religious affiliations; and a common characteristic that creates an unwillingness to compromise in order to collaborate. The Middle-Eastern nations continue to harbour independent views, political positions and threat perceptions even in the face of an adversary that questions the very legitimacy of these nations.

It is more than apparent that enormous power—military, economic and ideological—is required to defeat the IS and to effectively contain the violent insurgency that is bound to follow such a defeat. The necessary quantum of power necessary to achieve such an outcome is currently not available within the coalition and is unlikely to be generated in the near-term. The situation needs immediate, concerted and decisive action. Failure will see the rapid and domino-like collapse of the Arab nations, once the first one succumbs.

The Islamic State's Strategy

The military operations being undertaken by the IS is only part, albeit a critical one, of the overall strategy that it employs. Their operations erode the lines of distinction between terrorism, insurgency and conventional warfare, creating a new hybrid modus operandi that draws from the tactical aspects of each. The current military opposition to the IS emanates mainly from the Western coalition, which is carrying out only air strikes. The IS has adapted its operational tactics to cater for the preponderant air power that the coalition brings to bear. However, rolling back the IS from the territories that it occupies needs ground forces in combat, which has not happened effectively till now. The only worthwhile opponents on the ground have been the Kurdish forces although they receive very limited external assistance. However, this is only the operational side of the IS activities.

While the military conflict is important, the IS focus is on systematically attacking the idea of sovereign nation-states based on artificially drawn borders in the region. As a subset of this, they are intent on diffusing the concept of nationality, nationalism and patriotism as binding factors that maintain a state as a viable entity. For the time being the IS spotlight is on Iraq and Syria. Iraq for all practical purposes does not fit the description of a viable nation anymore and is permanently divided into Sunni, Shi'a and Kurdish enclaves or provinces. Syria is the battle ground for largest civil war the region has so far seen and its territory is controlled by a number of groups holding small areas. The limited national bonds that existed in the past have already been frayed in both these nations—with the sectarian violence that followed the ill-advised US invasion in Iraq; and with the civil war that erupted almost as a homage to the forgotten Arab-Spring in Syria.

The challenge to the idea of a nation-state is the fundamental difference in the IS doctrine from earlier Islamic groups and secular nationalists. Political Islam by itself is not a new phenomenon, it has been practised even before World War II by groups like the Muslim Brotherhood. However, these groups never challenged the concept of nation-states, instead they were patriots contesting for political legitimacy within the national space. Even in the question of nationalism, the Middle-East followed a different route to disenchantment. By the beginning of the Arab-Spring in 2010-11, nationalism and patriotism, as interpreted by the autocratic leaders who ruled the nations across the Middle-East, had lost much of its sheen to the general public. Even so, the Arab-Spring still functioned within the concept and constraints of a nation-state, clearly demonstrated by the very different outcomes that it achieved in Egypt, Tunisia, Iraq and Syria.

There are three elements that hold a nation together as an entity—visible state institutions; identifiable leadership; and palpable patriotism based on nationalism. At the very minimum, nationalism requires the people of the state to have an acceptance of a shared history as well as a believable narrative of a common and prosperous future. When two of the three elements fail simultaneously, the state fails, giving way to malicious sectarianism and instability. During the Arab-Spring in Tunisia and Egypt, state institutions and nationalism survived with only the leadership failing; the nations continued as recognisable entities. In both Iraq and Syria, the state institutions failed, an almost non-existent nationalism was blown away and only the leadership survived, leading the way to the chaos that is being witnessed. The IS was quick to take advantage of the fragile situation and project itself as a stable alternative.

The IS is rooted in a strong Islamic ideology that is based on fundamentalist interpretations of the religion and wages a direct war against the concept of a sovereign state based on nationalism. Its ultimate aim is to establish a Caliphate based on adherence to Islam instead of nationalism, through expanding the existing Sunni-Shi'a divide in the Muslim world. By concentrating on Iraq and Syria as the base for their activities the IS has cleverly picked on two nations of Western creation where the population has only a tentative appreciation of nationalism and perhaps very limited understanding of patriotism, mainly because of their having been long under repressive dictatorial rule. In combination with attempts to delegitimise the non-Islamic past through the destruction of ancient artefacts and other symbols, the IS aims to demonstrate the failure of nationalism as a viable social construct. Left unchecked, the ideological disruption could even overtake nations like Turkey and Egypt that have a very strong ethos of nationalism and patriotism.

Currently the IS controlled territory extends from north-west Syria to the western approaches to Baghdad and juts north till the borders of Iraqi Kurdistan. It has a de facto capital at Raqqa in Syria, and controls a total area of about 11,000 square miles, which is around the size of Belgium containing a population estimated to be around eight million. More importantly the IS provides a semblance of order in the territories that it controls, a welcome change from the complete chaos of the civil war. It has institutionalised taxes and levies that are collected by a cadre of administrative 'officers', and also provides civic amenities. The IS controlled areas have their power lines repaired and sewage systems cleaned while food security is enforced. They also run a regular bus service across the border between Iraq and Syria.

It is in the education system which has been instituted that the long term objectives of the IS becomes clearly visible. The curriculum is based on Islamic studies, jihadist ideology and military training to the complete exclusion of any other subject. There is also a deliberate attempt at brainwashing the next generation at an early age by teaching them fundamentalist Islamic thought and even encouraging them to spy on their parents and report them for anti-Muslim activities if the strictest version of the religion is not being practised at home. They are also desensitised to extreme violence by exposing them to beheadings and other callous acts against perceived enemies. By institutionalising a strict and severe order in places where anarchy has been the norm for decades the IS is creating a foundation to build further.

The provision of public services and strict governance is the first step towards state-creation and for the general population in areas where stability has been a forgotten factor for years, it has a certain attraction. In a telling proof, a recent survey saw that one in five Syrians within the IS territory preferred the IS to the previous regime. Under these circumstances the IS knows fully well that if the Assad regime is removed, they will be able to move in to fill the void. At the moment there are no 'moderate' leaders who have the military or political clout to take control of the broken state if regime change is on the cards. The state-building activities ensure the longevity of the IS despite being under almost continuous military, economic and political attack for more than a year.

It is wishful thinking that the IS will vanish as an identifiable entity if it is militarily defeated, or 'destroyed' as Western leadership states in high rhetoric. Further, the notion of restoring Iraq and Syria into viable states is purely utopian thinking; it is not going to happen. They are far too critically broken for any repair to be effective. The global and regional powers involved in this war against the IS have to move on beyond this repetitive mantra. The Western alignment, primarily military but also political to a certain extent, with Saudi Arabia and the Government of Iraq has so far not produced any tangible results. One of the main reasons is that Sunni jihadist sympathy is embedded in both Syria and Iraq, the central region of the conflict. Leveraging on this the IS has clearly stated its ideology and envisaged end-state and is further boosted by its success in state-creation. IS is seen as an outlet for Sunnis to express perceived grievances and injustice against them that in turn provides the organisation with long term validity.

It is also disturbing that so far the international discourse against the IS has been at the operational and tactical military levels whereas the IS themselves have always kept their narrative above this, concentrating on their overarching aim of creating a Caliphate with the military actions being only instrumental in this struggle. The opposition to the IS has so far failed to address the real issue at the strategic and ideological level. Military operations alone will never be able to surmount such a challenge.

Creating an Opposing Strategy

If the challenge or threat of the IS is to be comprehensively defeated, the West and its regional allies need to create and employ a holistic, integrated and sustainable strategy. Currently there is only a military operational concept in place, that too a disjointed one since all the coalition members do not share a common belief in the desired end-state or a common understanding of how to achieve it. Even the military operations, in its current form, could at best contain further territorial spread of the IS, but will not be able to stop them from getting entrenched in their current territorial holdings. Dislodging the IS will require the employment of significant ground forces, which seems unlikely to take place at this juncture. Even if a ground campaign is envisaged, the forces would have to be regional and not 'western' multi-national, a situation highly unlikely to happen unless the regional powers start to be directly threatened.

The fickleness of Western support to the groups fighting the IS on the ground has been another factor in making the defeat of the IS difficult. The Kurds have so far been the only group who have defeated the IS on the ground. However, their supply lines are becoming strained because of the Western need to placate Turkey in order to use Turkish airbases. This backtracking from support to the Kurds may be explained away as pragmatism, but does not make operational sense. Although a member of NATO, it is difficult to consider Turkey as anything other than an unhelpful ally and therefore the urgency to appease Turkish 'preciousness' is not understandable. But that is the situation of the ground at the moment. The Kurds with long memories must be squirming with a sense of déjà vu.

The challenge of IS is one of ideas and ideology, one that threatens regional stability well into the future if not effectively dealt with now; the military action is only a tool. The IS already is displaying its ability to recruit Sunni Arab citizens to its fold, although the Sunni nations of the region do not seem to be aware of the seriousness of the situation. The Middle-Eastern nations participating in the war consider the removal of Bashar al Assad from power as a higher priority than the defeat of the IS. In the bargain they are still indirectly supporting the growth of the IS. This situation needs elaboration. Saudi Arabia continues to believe that Assad and the Syrian crisis created the IS and that the group will vanish when Assad has been deposed. Saudi Arabia and other Arab countries ignore the gradual radicalisation of the unemployed youth in their countries. This imperceptible change has been the result of decades of misguided foreign policies, repressive and exclusionary domestic strategies, and the capricious rule of visibly corrupt and self-indulgent autocrats. The so-called regional powers have not understood that the current situation has been the result of their own ostrich-like attitude and support to both regional and global Sunni extremism.

The current alternatives to the growing stature of the IS are the existing autocracies where the rulers have no apparent stake in the societies that they rule. These autocrats cannot conclusively prove to their people that they are the better of the two evils since repression of peaceful attempts at participation in governance, and in extremis regime change, has been the norm in these countries. The heavy-handed actions against the nascent Arab Spring activities have played into the hands of the IS, boosting their appeal. The current debate is only regarding how to contain and then defeat the IS, at a military level. This ignores the fact that military initiatives aligned to achieve a 'contain and defeat' outcome will not lead to any lasting victory over the amorphous entity that is IS.

Defeat, in its classic interpretation, can only be meted out to a conventional military force of a sovereign nation. History demonstrates that 'defeated' religious and/or ideological movements almost always rise, phoenix-like, from the ashes of their defeat better adapted to survive than before. The contradictory aims being pursued by the West and its allies in the military campaign further dilutes the possibility of a military defeat of the IS in the near future.

Following containment as a strategy brings a completely different facet to the war. It will be a tacit acceptance of the IS as a state and that jihadism has not been defeated in more than two decades of military operations. The strategy of containment will have to be developed in two distinct parts—the physical and the ideological. Its success will depend on both the parts functioning together. Physical containment requires the coalition to create a watertight geographic area from within which the IS is not permitted to move, establish external contact or receive any assistance. A porous border will not serve the purpose. Ideological containment will depend on the ability of the coalition to provide an alternative narrative to counter the religious doctrine currently propagated by the IS. The employment of this strategy will be similar to the Cold War situation when democracy and individual freedom were placed as the viable alternatives to communism and collective socialism. At the moment such an ideological or religious alternative is not available to the floundering youth who are flocking to the IS. However, such an alternative narrative will have to be provided by the nations of the Middle-East if it is to gain traction and taken seriously. The regional powers will need to change their attitude towards the IS, which they clandestinely support while overtly opposing in official statements.

In order to develop a practical strategy it is necessary to appreciate the IS appeal to the people of Iraq and Syria—they provide the only ray of hope for stability in times of utmost despair. The support to IS is only partially because of a belief in their ideology, but mainly because of the lack of a viable alternative. Therefore, a successful strategy can only be built by creating a sustainable and credible alternative that opposes the public brutality and a governance system based on archaic interpretations of Islamic scriptures and medieval theological pronouncements. The religious tenets of Islam that are being twisted and misinterpreted by the IS must be rationally and ethically analysed and explained in a manner that cannot and will not be confused as anti-Muslim bigotry. Only then will the myths that the IS is perpetuating as religious sanction for its barbaric behaviour be disputed and debunked. A workable strategy to counter the IS will have to build back confidence in the concept of a nation state and nationalism through a number of initiatives. The confidence building will have to be undertaken through regional cooperation, and altering the public perception of the role of the nation in creating law and order to establish stability. These initiatives will have to be buttressed by international assistance to the nations that are likely to become increasingly fragile. Unlike the two already failed nations—Iraq and Syria— no other country in the region must be allowed to fail as a nation state.

A piecemeal approach through a combination of military actions and ideological dialogue is unlikely to work in thwarting the IS moves. The current approach of incrementally attempting to control the IS through countering their initiatives will only squander available strategic options and strengthen the group. Rigorous containment—both physical and ideological—and a clear and demonstrated definition of the ideological alternative is the only way to deprive the IS of its religious and revolutionary attraction. Military victory in this war will not defeat the IS. They can only be metaphorically starved into insignificance leading to a gradual fall into oblivion, which is the only long term solution. Does the opposition have the wherewithal to create, and steadfastly employ such a complex strategy for the long term?

Conclusion

The IS is not a terrorist organisation that can be defeated by traditional and outdated anti-terrorism methods. Irrespective of what the ruling house of Saudi Arabia might say, that the IS is neither Islamic nor a state, it has to be accepted that the IS is a state based on religion and with a standing army. It is also a movement nourished by an extreme and violent version of religion thriving on an anachronistic interpretation of religious dogma. The IS takes advantage of a fractured society with almost no cohesive nationalism through a cynical, opportunistic and abusive interpretation of religious ideology that creates a sense of integration.

The concept and pursuance of a modern-day Caliphate is a serious threat to the countries of the Middle-East. In order to counter the spread of IS, the first step will have to be a political solution to the Syrian Civil War facilitated by both Western, Russian and regional assistance and commitment. This will be the only way to starve the IS of its physical and ideological support base. Thereafter the national power elements of the countries of the region—economic, political and military—should be brought to bear with a non-sectarian religious ideology visibly superimposed on them. The IS can be rooted out only by the people living in the territories that it holds and to do this they need all the assistance that they can get from the regional powers. The military campaign and ideological counterattack are battles for the regional powers to fight and win, not outsiders. Running away is not resistance, it fractures the cohesion of people facing a calamitous situation; staying and fighting is the only way forward.

Published in Eurasia Review 22 September 2015

http://www.eurasiareview.com/22092015-the-islamic-state-understanding-and-countering-its-strategy-analysis/

11

RUSSIA IN THE MIDDLE-EAST
ALTERING THE GEOSTRATEGIC
ENVIRONMENT

I n the second half of September, Russia moved military forces predominated by air assets, into Bassel al-Assad international airport in the Latakia province of Syria. This deployment made it impossible for the anti-Assad forces to capture the province and also provided a logistics lifeline to the military forces of the Syrian president, Bashar al-Assad. An-124 transport aircraft and landing ships from Russia's Black Sea fleet started to deliver equipment to the beleaguered Syrian forces. The same supply chain could also be servicing the Hezbollah forces supporting the Assad regime. On 30 September, the Russian military forces started air attacks on targets in the anti-Assad rebel-held territories. By this action Russia demonstrated its expanding political and military influence in the Middle-East and its will to initiate decisive action.

The Russian initiative complicates the situation where the US-led Western coalition is already undertaking a complex air campaign. The Russians are targeting not only the Islamic State (IS) but also all other anti-Assad rebel/jihadist forces, some of whom are directly affiliated to the Western coalition, some even trained and supplied by the US. Although a direct confrontation between the US and Russia is highly unlikely, it confuses the battlespace even further. There is speculation that Russian air activity is a precursor to the Russian army commencing a joint counter-attack along with Syrian forces, which would mean a more direct involvement for the Russian military. If this comes to pass, the Russian Army would be clashing with the US-supplied and trained Free Syrian Army—a situation fraught with the risk of escalating consequences.

A ground campaign will also create a situation where Russia may not be able to avoid mission creep; although it will provide greater flexibility to the overall campaign and provide the ability to scale up or down as required.

Russia's Objectives

From the start of the Syrian Civil War four years ago, Russia has articulated the need for the survival of the Assad regime to enable a peaceful political transition. In the past few months a controlled regime transition has become the steadfast aim of Russian political, diplomatic and military initiatives. While the survival of the regime is indeed the priority objective, it is a short-term goal, the survival of the Syrian state as an entity being the ultimate aim. Essentially Russia is protecting its national interests: first, Assad is being supported to be used later as a bargaining tool when the inevitable regime change has to take place as and when the volatile situation has been stabilised; and second, Russia will not give up the naval base at Tartus, the only Russian base in the Mediterranean and critical to power projection. By protecting the Assad regime from the current onslaught, Russia is also ensuring that it has a decisive role in determining the future of Syria—with or without Assad at the helm—and thereby becoming the most influential power broker in the region.

Towards this end Russia has entered into an understanding on intelligence sharing with Syria, Iraq and Iran, clearly indicating that it will not let Assad be removed in a hurry. The move took the US and its allies completely by surprise. There is an unstated understanding that the current regime has to transition to a new rule sometime in the not too distant future. Russia wants to control the timing and the modality of such a transition and also have a deciding vote on who will succeed Bashar al-Assad as the leader of the fractured State. It knows that in any negotiated settlement Assad will have an influential position and therefore Assad must remain beholden to Russia at all times. Bashar al-Assad has revealed himself to be a ruthless pragmatist and will play a transitional role that suits Russia, but is likely to drive a hard bargain for his acceptance of regime change when the time comes. However, that eventuality is far into the future, at least for now. With the Russian intervention, the strategic situation has evolved considerably and Russia is clearly implementing a dynamic strategy, the better to protect its interests.

Russia knows that a fully negotiated settlement will only eventuate, if at all, at a much later date and that event then there is no surety of the deal holding in the long-term. It therefore wants to hedge its bets and broaden the target-base and attack all jihadists, irrespective of whether they have been classified 'good' and/or 'moderates'. Smarting under the US and Western enforced sanctions, Russia has carefully crafted a plan to use the Syrian conflict, which the West has not been able to prosecute effectively, to return to the international arena as an influential global power. This is the first step in its calculated move to break out of the Western imposed sanctions and engage with other nations involved in the conflict. The Syrian Civil War has from the beginning been a quagmire, with it becoming increasingly unfathomable as to who is fighting whom and for what. Conflicting national, regional and global interests have become intertwined with irreconcilable sectarian, religious and ideological doctrine.

By initiating decisive action and taking a direct role in the conflict to steadfastly support the Assad regime, Russia has clearly shown the difference between its approach and that of the US, which has been dogged by ambiguity of strategy and changing strategic aims. Like a chess Grand Master at his best, President Putin has aligned his pieces on the board in such a way that the US-led coalition can no longer act alone and ensured that the Islamic State can only be defeated with Russian participation. Isolating Russia is no longer an option for the West. Russia has also guaranteed that Assad's post-war role is not negotiable—the choices in front of US has suddenly narrowed.

Conflicting Views

The US and Russia have opposing viewpoints regarding the Assad regime although some commonality of ultimate aims in the Syrian Civil War are also noticeable. The US sees Bashar al-Assad as the source of the current conflict and as providing the jihadist elements an opening into the Levant. It believes that removing Assad will be the first step towards resolution of the crisis. Considering the recent history of the region in Iraq and Libya, this is a rather naïve appraisal of the situation. Russia on the other hand considers Assad as a bulwark against the further spread of the jihadist groups, a diametrically opposing view and perhaps closer to the truth than is being admitted by the Western coalition.

Even though the short-term goals are at odds with each other, both the US and Russia agree that defeating the IS is a prerequisite for the success of any negotiated transition of political authority in Syria, even though the reasons vary slightly. The IS is a direct threat to Russia with its declaration of the

Islamic Caliphate that includes the volatile North Caucasus, already home to a violent jihadist separation movement. Additionally, there are an estimated 1700 Russians fighting in the army of the IS who could return home to foment trouble. The US is opposed to the IS more in an altruistic manner than as a direct threat to the homeland, at least for the present. However, there is no reason that the US and Russian strategic aims cannot be reconciled and aligned.

It has to be accepted that the current strategy of the Western coalition is unlikely to produce the desired end-state in the Syrian conflict. When viewed in a detached manner, three factors come out very clearly as being fundamental to altering the strategy in order to pave the way towards a sustainable stability. One, functioning governance by local authorities must be established in the areas that are not IS-controlled, including the areas that are still under Assad's control, in order to improve the credibility of the non-IS factions. Two, enforceable attack free zones within the Syrian borders, where no party is able to attack or coerce the civilian population, must be created. This will be the first step towards ensuring stability that should gradually spread. Three, the Western coalition and the Russian group should negotiate and create a common military strategy to win the war and subsequently to stabilise the future. This can only happen if the US accepts firstly that Assad has a role to play in the transition phase and secondly the importance of Russia as an influential, and perhaps even controlling, factor of the Assad regime.

After the Russian intervention, the options available to the US-led coalition reduced drastically. In fact the only viable solution to stabilise a situation that is spiralling out of control will come from arriving at an understanding for military cooperation, which should then lead to the creation of an effective coalition that involves the regional nations including both Saudi Arabia and Iran. This might sound far-fetched, considering the pervasive hostility between some of the regional countries, but is achievable if both the US and Russia are willing to pressurise their allies to do so. Within this scenario, Assad has to stay in power for the near term to ensure an orderly transfer of power after the IS has been defeated. This three step process is the only way that the IS can be defeated and the region brought back to normalcy.

Not far behind the Syrian imbroglio is the question of Iraq, which is also violently unstable at the moment. The West's relationship with Iraq vis-à-vis the Iranian influence is vexed. Even so, Iraq has given tacit support for Assad because of the belief that his removal in the current circumstances will only strengthen the IS. Iraq has also permitted Russia to use its airspace to transport weapons and equipment to Syria and even gone to the extent of declaring that it would not be averse to Russian air attacks on IS elements operating in Iraqi territory. There is a definitive feeling that Iraq is cautiously moving away from the stranglehold of US influence.

Impact on the Region and Participants

The Russian initiative has created both short-term and far-reaching consequences for the participants in the conflict as well as for other nations in the region. Israel is the one nation that is not participating directly in the conflict but has constantly involved itself in attempting to steer the course of events as far as possible. Ever since the break-up of the Soviet Union, the Israel-Russia relationship has been complex with both nations regularly meddling in each other's spheres of influence. Israel has managed to cultivate strong military-technological relations with a number of former Soviet States. Almost in return, Russia has staunchly supported Iran and Syria—nations that are inimical to Israel and its perceived security needs. However, both Russia and Israel have maintained an acceptable level of reasoned cordiality in their dealings with each other. Israel is a pragmatic nation with a clear long-term view of its place in the Middle-East and the risks and challenges that it faces. It is not difficult to imagine that Israel and Russia could arrive at a mutually agreed, beneficial security deal.

Turkey's Dilemma

The Russian air campaign creates impossible complications for Turkey's strategy to emerge from this conflict as a stronger and more influential player in the region. Turkey's ultimate aim is to create a pliant Sunni-led Syria that functions fully within Turkey's own sphere of influence. The critical factor in achieving this is the removal of Assad from power and hence the concerted support to anti-Assad forces and also turning a blind eye to IS activities for a long period of time. The Russian support for Assad through the conduct of an air campaign directly negates Turkish ambitions to create a no-fly 'safe' zone in Syrian territory contiguous to its own. A brief background is necessary to understand the implications of recent actions by both nations.

In June 2012, a reconnaissance Phantom of the Turkish Air Force was shot down by Syrian air defence forces. Turkey immediately changed the rules of engagement and started to carryout intrusive interceptions of Syrian Air

Force aircraft coming even remotely close to their border. With the start of the air campaign, the reported Russian air violations into Turkish airspace takes on a new meaning. While Russia has dismissed these violations as navigational errors compounded by bad weather, they will have to be seen as a test of Turkey's ability and will to enforce the changed rules of engagement. Ankara is being dared and is on show.

Turkey under President Erdogan is facing a foreign policy debacle, compounded by the Russian intervention. After being recalcitrant, it opened its air bases to the Western coalition calculating that by doing so it would achieve two objectives—one, that it would hasten the fall of the Assad regime; and two, that it would facilitate Turkey's own efforts to counter the Kurdish advance along its border with Syria. Defeating the IS is not a priority for Turkey, which declared it a terrorist group only in September 2014. However, Russia now stands as an unmoving obstacle to Turkey's foreign policy ambitions. After a recent Erdogan-Putin meeting there was no joint statement made, which is an ominous diplomatic speak for stating that there is 'respectful' disagreement between the two nations on matters that were discussed. Russia will not provide even diplomatic support for Turkey's ambitions regarding the future of Syria, since their own ambition is at odds with that of Turkey. In the meantime Turkey has taken up the fight against the Kurdish groups—the Kurdish Democratic Union Party (PYD) in Syria and the Kurdistan Workers Party (PKK) in Turkey—with the real risk of these actions escalating into a full-fledged Turkish civil war. Turkey is suddenly left with very limited alternatives.

Another irksome factor for Turkey is that Russia has become the de facto guarantor-power for the security of Azerbaijan, a nation that has so far been a close ally of Turkey. The strong bilateral relationship that Turkey shared with Russia, especially the personal friendship between Erdogan and Putin, has been buffeted by the deep differences that have surfaced regarding the future of Syria. The visions are at complete odds with each other. Diplomatic cordiality has now been stretched to the limit and could snap at any time. In these tense times, it only needs a single catalyst for overt animosity to crystallise. At the moment building the pipeline that was to carry Russian gas to Turkey has been kept on hold, an indication of the changed geo-strategic situation.

The United States

Russia-US relations were at an all-time low after Russian interference in Ukraine and the subsequent Western sanctions that were imposed on Russia. Russia believes that the intervention in Ukraine and the annexation of Crimea were legitimate actions initiated to secure Russian interests. In this event, it is not surprising that Russia considers the US to be its chief rival. The US-led coalition's lack of an articulated strategy to stabilise Syria is seen by Russia as an opportunity to restart a common purpose dialogue with the US, which could subsequently lead to regular bilateral talks and gradual normalisation of relationship. The fact that the US has indirectly indicated that it is not too particular about the time-frame of Assad's departure, as long as a deliberate and orderly transition plan that will be executed at some future date exists.

In Syria and the fight against the IS, the US has painted itself into a corner. It supported the Free Syrian Army, labelling it the moderate opposition, whose intended aim was to oust the Assad regime. Through a $500 million program run out of Turkey to train soldiers for this 'moderate' group, the US was able to produce inly 75 soldiers for insertion into Syria, most of whom scattered at the first sign of the IS with some of them 'donating' their weapons and equipment to the al Qaeda elements in Syria. With the IS continuing to further their single-minded focus to create an Islamic Caliphate, getting rid of Assad has slowly, but surely, been moved down the list of prioritised objectives by the US. It is soft-pedalling the initial demand for regime change. There is thinking that the long-term requirement to remove Assad from power could be achieved with Russia-led negotiations after the defeat of the IS. That the Russians are currently targeting the so-called moderates is now being considered, at least in some quarters of the strategy development area in the US, as a minor inconvenience. So much for the reliability of the US regarding support to friends and allies. Russia's long-term goals of keeping Ukraine within its circle of influence and getting the economic sanctions lifted just got a fillip with the air campaign in Syria.

The US and Russia have now signed a memorandum of understanding on air safety in the Syrian airspace to minimise the risk of in-flight incidents. The agreement specifies safety protocols, the use of specific communication frequencies and the setting up of a working group to ensure smooth implementation. This is tacit acceptance by the Western coalition that the Russian Air Force cannot be willed away from the battle zone.

Europe

It is in its dealings with Europe that Russia's frustrations at the loss of super power status manifests with great intensity. The loss of influence in the 'near abroad' of the Soviet era through the expansion of NATO and the transformative power of the European Union (EU) is anathema to the spread of Russian power and the nationalistic fervour of its leadership. A united Europe is a potential threat to Russian ambition and therefore, Putin's strategic goal is to divide, disrupt and interrupt any policy initiatives aimed at achieving some semblance of unity. The creation of energy projects that would pit European nations against each other is one of the moves that facilitates and perpetuates this approach.

Russia's Syrian initiative is connected to the volatile situation in Ukraine. With the US and Europe pre-occupied with Syria, there is relative calm in Ukraine where the Russia-backed opposition is growing stronger and consolidating its position. Further, the Russian air campaign also has the potential to create dissonance between the US and Europe, especially with the unforeseen refugee crisis that has enveloped Europe, which in turn has increased the terrorist threat in broader Europe. European governments are becoming increasingly anxious and some have even indicated their support for ground intervention. Willingness to put boots-on-the-ground is clear indication of the enormity of the challenge that they face. Europe's view of Assad is altering with him playing a limited role in the transition process becoming acceptable along with a tacit acceptance of the pivotal role that Russia is likely to play in any such political transition. The US non-success in defeating the IS after more than a year has eroded its credibility and has assisted Putin in his attempt to create European support for his actions in the Middle-East.

The anti-Russian sanctions are expensive and a divisive effort for the European nations who have a long-standing desire to rebuild trade with Russia. Moscow is craftily posing itself as an alternative source of power to Washington and Brussels, playing directly to populist anti-EU parties in most European nations. The aim is to further create disharmony in trans-Atlantic relationships. Russian activities in the Middle-East must not be viewed purely within the geographical boundaries of that region, but strategically in an overarching manner, with an understanding of the angst that Russia suffered immediately after the collapse of the Soviet Union that led to the loss of status and power and its very long term aim to once again becoming a global power. Europe is clearly in Russia's sights.

Saudi Arabia

It is a tense time in Russia-Arab relations. Saudi Arabia has taken few tentative steps towards improving its relationship with Russia by arriving at some agreements on economic cooperation, a move that led to speculations regarding the Saudi-US relations being in the doldrums. However, Saudi Arabia wants Russia to moderate its support for the Assad regime, especially since it supports anti-Assad forces being targeted by the Russian air campaign. There is an inherent risk in this situation since Russian air strikes could lead to inadvertent and unintended military confrontation. The Saudi monarchy is caught in a cleft stick in terms of available options; with the US ability, and perhaps more importantly, reliability, to keep regional opponents in check coming increasingly under a cloud; and the underlying belief that negotiating a full deal on Syria with Russia may lead to unknown and unpredictable consequences both in the short and long term. The US is running out of policy options to placate Saudi Arabia and may not be able to bring it back fully into the American orbit.

For Russia, Saudi Arabia could also turn out to be the joker in the pack. Russia will not have forgotten that Saudi Arabia was the prime mover in its Afghanistan debacle in the 1980s and even now provide support, both materiel and financial, to the Islamic rebels in Russia. It was also Saudi Arabian charities that financed the Chechen rebels in the 1990s. Saudi clerics have already started to paint the Russian intervention in shades of religious hue, calling it a new 'Christian Crusade' against Islam. It is also possible that the Gulf nations could ramp up their support for rebel groups that are operating in the lawless Iraq-Syria region. However, Russia has cautioned the major Arab nations against supplying the jihadists with man-portable air defence systems, which they have said will be a red line, never to be crossed. The questions remain: will the Saudis create and lead a coalition to remove Assad from power, irrespective of the state of the war against the IS? And, if such a situation comes to pass, how will Russia react? Will it start a greater conflagration in the region that could subsume even non-participants in one unholy fire?

Geo-Strategic Implications

First and foremost, it has to be squarely recognised that there has been an inexorable failure of Western strategy in controlling the initial Syrian Civil War and its subsequent explosive expansion through the activities of the IS. The US has so far instituted only half-measures that have not shown any indication of success. The Russian intervention creates a small window of opportunity to initiate a long-term strategy to achieve a political solution. Russia has taken over the Syrian air base from which it can undertake missions across the entire Levant and Eastern Mediterranean and the naval base that gives it unfettered naval access to the Mediterranean Sea. It has also expanded the ground facilities and turned the air base into a major Russian base, indicating an intent for protracted use. Effectively this creates a permanent Russian footprint in the Middle-East with the ability to project power into the Arab world. The foundation for the quest for global status is gradually being laid.

Russia will protect the Assad regime, at least for the near-term, with all its resources. It will demonstrate effectiveness in its campaign and may even try to create another coalition with Syria, the Lebanese Hezbollah, Iraq and Iran to counter the Western coalition. The Iraqi government has already consented to Russian use of its airspace while the Russian air operations constrain the uninhibited freedom of operations that the Western coalition had so far enjoyed. The violations of Turkish airspace and the reaction that it has provoked increases the chances of miscalculations spiralling out of control. The violations could also be considered probing missions that were meant to test NATO's ability and willingness to invoke Article V that provides collective defence provisions for member nations, since Turkey is a member. Russian air activity is a serious blow to the credibility of the Western coalition.

Some strategists have opined that Russia is implementing the concept of 'reflexive control', a concept built on effectively shaping the environment in such a manner that the adversary is forced to choose a course of action that one wants it to choose, and is ready to counter. The decreasing effectiveness of the Western coalition and their unstated acceptance of the role that the Assad regime will play in a future power transition is a manifestation of this concept. There is already an informal Russia-Syria-Iran axis that has formed making it necessary for the US-led coalition to fundamentally reassess their geo-strategic alignment. The facts on the ground is that Syria has already been geographically partitioned and there is no reason to believe that the country will return to its pre-war boundaries as a single entity—that is an impossibility. The next phase of the Civil War, which Russia controls, will eventually shape the contour of the region.

The long-term stability of the region is dependent on the ability of the intervening forces to settle the simmering discord in Libya, Iraq and Syria, all created by Western interference and wayward use of force. Russian viewpoint is that there are no jihadist groups that can be termed as moderate and that the difference between them is only their degree of affinity to the IS. All of them have to be treated as terrorists. The Russians have clearly, and cleverly, divided the conflict into Assad versus the rest. Russia has also demonstrated its strategic will to initiate decisive action with a willingness to take and accept risks. At the operational level, the Russian Air Force is functioning under a much more relaxed set of rules of engagement than the Western coalition, which could make a tangible difference in the war against the IS. So far the US and Russia have managed to de-conflict their missions and moves. However, the downside is that despite the flight safety agreements there is no assurance that a wrong tactical action that could lead to a confrontation at the operational level will not be made. This is the reason for some analysts to assert that the Russian intervention will create further geo-strategic disorder.

Russia is now engaged in a long-term game of patience, perseverance and persistence, willing to wait even for the next US administration to take charge and settle down more than 15 months later. It has three strategic objectives to secure. First is emphasising the sanctity and legitimacy of a sovereign government and the non-acceptance of external intervention to effect regime change. Second is to demonstrate Russia's steadfastness in supporting its friends, in sharp contrast to the track record of the US who is seen to have abandoned its friends at will. Russia wants to be seen as a better ally than the US. However, this could become a double-edged sword. Political inconsistency and nuanced double-standards may not be avoidable in global diplomacy, especially in the prevailing volatile circumstances and Russia might find itself in the same position as the US in the future. This might become apparent to Russia only when it becomes as involved in international politics and interventions as the US has been in the past two decades.

Third, Russia wants to emerge from this conflict as the protector of the minorities in the greater Middle-East. With the IS rampaging across the region, the minorities have lost faith in the ability of the West to protect them and believe that on a number of occasions they have been sacrificed to radical Islam and/or totalitarianism. The IS has deepened the sectarian schism in the Middle-East far beyond at any other time in history. Russia believes that it can use the minorities to create an enhanced Russian influence in the region. This could involve direct involvement of Iran in the endeavour since Russian national interests are more aligned with Iran than with any other nation.

Russia is pragmatic enough to accept that the only way to end this conflict is through a negotiated political settlement. However, the collective defeat of the IS is fundamental to any progress in the political front and such a defeat cannot be achieved by a conditional fight against it. Russia's advantage is that it is the only entity that has the influence to make Assad compromise and accept a negotiated settlement. Even so, it wants Assad to come to the negotiation table from a position of strength, although he currently controls only about 20 per cent of the country. There is also no chance of bringing the old Syria together without engaging in a bloody and protracted ground war. A future Syria can at best be a federation of quasi-independent states—controlled by Kurds, Alawites, Sunnis and Druze—the Civil War has gone too far to even hope for a reconciled country to emerge.

It is early days as yet in the renewed conflict with Russia flexing its muscle and there is still no indication regarding how long the conflict will drag on into the future. However, Russia has indicated that it wants the other regional nations, Saudi Arabia and Turkey, to be part of the negotiations regarding Syria's future while it plays the role of the arbitrator. Saudi Arabia at least seems to be inching towards acceptance of a transition period with Assad continuing to be part of the equation. In a subtle diplomatic move it has indicated that it does not rule out talks with Iran and is conscious that it needs to continue the dialogue with US, Russia and Turkey who are the other major stake holders in the war.

It is revealing that some Western analysts have been quick to denounce Russian intervention as having been made in haste with no exit strategy. This accusation indicates the height of hypocrisy, since they seem to have forgotten that the US and its allies has not been able to articulate an exit strategy from the Middle-East for the past 14 years. The Russian action immediately exposed the bankruptcy of the US non-strategy and empty diplomatic rhetoric. The US has irrevocably damaged its reputation through fickle and ill-conceived diplomacy, injudicious employment of its mighty military forces, failed attempts at supporting a number of local forces—the list of failures is long. It is likely that the US may have abdicated the leadership of the region by default. This is a self-created vacuum of power and nature abhors a vacuum. Russia seems to be willingly stepping up to fill the emerging vacuum.

Conclusion

The Russian military intervention in the Syrian Civil War reveals two visible failures of Western, read US, policies—first, of isolating and punishing Russian for the actions that were initiated in Ukraine; and second, placing regime change as a precondition for the success of the Syrian intervention. The Western coalition, beset with weak and indecisive leadership, lacks the moral authority to ensure success even though billions of dollars have already been expended with very little to show for it. Russia has entered the fray cautiously and not without calculating the pitfalls as some people claim. Its action should be seen as reinforcing its veto in the UN Security Council with actions on the ground that metaphorically amounts to another veto. From a Russian viewpoint the air campaign in Syria is only one part of a greater 'war' being conducted to increase its influence in the global political environment.

For some obtuse reason, the Western coalition, including its Arab allies, seem to think that the removal of the Assad regime would in itself miraculously create a moderate alternative leadership that is entrenched in democratic values. This is delusional fantasy, if ever there was one. There is no doubt that Assad has been ruthless in his attempts to suppress the rebellion and may even be susceptible to charges of war crimes, but he has never been a threat to the broader region or a destabilising force for the outside world. The IS on the other hand is a barbaric, inhuman and philistine group that poses the biggest threat to normalcy that has so far emerged and is dedicated to the creation of a global Islamic Caliphate. The question that the Western coalition and Russia should be asking in concert is whether or not it is possible to build an all-inclusive grand coalition against the IS to ensure its defeat and destruction.

If such a coalition is to be built and be successful, certain preconditions will have to be accepted by all parties. First, Assad will have to be accepted at least as the lesser of the two evils necessary for short-term continuity of governance in order to avoid creating another Libya. Regime change will have to wait for the right time. Second at the operational level, there will be no creating of a no-fly zone in Syrian territory; there will be no ground incursions from the Turkish side of the border, even in hot pursuit; and there will be no air strikes on Assad-held sites in Syria. With the misleading confusion regarding which nation is openly or clandestinely supporting which jihadist group, it may be impossible to make the participating nations with their increasingly differing objectives subscribe to the Russian belief that there are no god or bad rebels or jihadists. However, distinguishing jihadists in such a manner is an ideological cul de sac, a dead end, and should not be pursued any further.

As it stands at the time of writing the US seems to be merely hoping that Putin fails, which unfortunately is not much of a policy option. However, who holds a stronger suite of cards is debatable and unclear although it looks as if the US will have to accept the inevitability of Assad being at least part of the initial solution in the political transition, whenever that takes place. The Sunni-ruled autocracies of the region could be coerced by the US and Russia to swallow this bitter pill to create the scene for longer-term stability, but by the same token, the reprieve might be short-lived. The sectarian divide in the region is far too deep to be papered over by coercion.

In the Middle-East for some time now, secularism has been confused with democracy much to the detriment of stability. Secularism, irrespective of the type of government, is a dire necessity in the region—unfortunately a utopian concept under the current circumstances. But unadulterated secularism may well be an ideal to be placed on the table lest the concept itself is lost.

Putin is acting to advance Russian interests and to protect his nation, which cannot be considered to be totally wrong actions whichever way one looks at it. Russia is purely pursuing the practical issue of national security. If the Russian intervention leads to stabilisation in Syria and Iraq Russia will achieve a monumental increase in its influence, prestige and status in the region as well as in the global geo-strategic environment. Getting unintentionally enmeshed in the sectarian fights of the region through mission creep remains the biggest risk to Russian intervention and will no doubt influence its future strategies.

Published in the Eurasia Review on 21 October 2015

http://www.eurasiareview.com/21102015-russia-in-the-middle-east-altering-the-geostrategic-environment-analysis/

12

TURKEY – AT A CRITICAL JUNCTURE

The 2002 electoral victory of the Justice and Development Party (*Adalet ve Kalkinma Partisi* or AKP) was a turning point in modern Turkey's political narrative. The relatively young leadership of the party, while subscribing to the secular basis of the Turkish Republic, was openly demonstrative of their devout Muslim identity and clearly articulated their support for the preservation of Islamic values and norms in society and the loosening of state control on religious practices. The international observers believed that this was the moment when Turkey would emerge to prove the compatibility of Islam and democracy to the wider Muslim world. However, an analysis of the state of Turkey after AKP has been in power for 13 years and is set to rule for another four, produces a somewhat different picture.

While the secular basis of the social and political order has not been dismantled, the framework has been eroded and is now brittle. There is also no denying that the social and political atmosphere has been irrevocably altered by the open permission and encouragement to use greater religious symbolism and imagery in all walks of life. More damaging has been the party's disregard for the norms of liberal democratic traditions. President Recep Tayyip Erdogan, the unquestioned 'king' of AKP, has revealed himself to be willing and ruthlessly able to silence and even persecute his opponents and critics, both within and outside his party. The authoritarian streak within the AKP leadership was exemplified by the jailing and sentencing of hundreds of military officers and other critics of the party on trumped up charges. The sanctity of the rule of law, and the democratic culture of the nation has been irrevocably damaged over the past decade.

The November 2015 Elections

Turkey went to the polls on 7 June 2015 and returned an ambiguous verdict, not giving any single party the necessary majority to rule. The election also brought the single party rule of the AKP to and end after 13 years. The reasons for this setback to AKP are many and varied, but it set in motion a series of events that could see Turkey transform into an entity that its founding father Mustafa Kemal would never be able to recognise. Turkey's constitution stipulates that in the event of a hung-election and the inability of any coalition to garner the numbers to rule, the country will have go back to the polls after a few months. This is exactly what happened—Turkey went back to the polls on 1 November and returned with a very different verdict as compared to 7 June. What happened between June and November to alter the public perception that now gives the AKP a fourth consecutive term?

The first noticeable change was the erosion of the sense of security that the people of Turkey had so far felt under the AKP. The upsurge in terrorism—with the bloody clashes against the Kurdistan Workers' Party (*Partiya Karkeren Kurdistane* or PKK) and the suicide bombings by the Islamic State (IS)—during the four months has spread an overall sense of diminished security in the country. The second was the economic downturn, not the result of the resurgence of political violence, but because of a certain amount of mismanagement and as a repercussion of flawed foreign policy initiatives. The Western media squarely blames President Erdogan for both these issues. However, the popular domestic view has been that these emerging issues are the result of the absence of a strong AKP government since the elections in 7 June.

This dichotomy has to be analysed further to arrive at a reasoned understanding of the situation. Before the June election, the priority issue for the nation was state of the economy, which was showing signs of wear and tear and in a downturn. The eruption of violence and terrorist attacks in the interim between the two elections was cleverly used by the AKP to point towards their previous record of 13 years of stability and convince the electorate that only a majority AKP government could solve the challenge posed to the nation through terrorism and violence. The fact is that although the economic indicators have not changed, even a little bit, between the two elections terrorism replaced economy on centre-stage in the election rhetoric. The majority Sunni electorate was convinced by the regime that the PKK had reignited fresh violence after June. The opposition indirectly assisted this explanation by being dysfunctional and not being able put forward a clear narrative of on-going events. The media played a significant role in influencing the popular perceptions regarding what was ailing the country.

On 1 November, the AKP won 49.4 per cent of the vote, an increase from the 40.9 per cent in June, capturing 316 of the 550 parliamentary seats, which is a comfortable majority. This result went against the grain of all predictions, to a certain extent even by the party itself. The National Action Party (*Milliyetci Hareket Partisi* or MHP) had won 80 seats and 16.4 per cent of the vote in June. However, it steadfastly refused to join the AKP in a coalition to form the government although both the parties have a broadly similar right wing, conservative outlook. This cost the party dearly in November, the people who were fed up of political instability punished the MHP. The party just managed to win 11.9 per cent of the vote and were reduced 40 seats in November. They are no longer an influential party in the Parliament.

The pro-Kurdish Peoples Democratic Party (*Halkalarin Demokratik Partisi* or HDP) had won double its traditional share of votes in June and managed to enter the parliament for the first time with 13.1 per cent of the votes and 80 seats. In November they managed to stay in the parliament, (Turkish electoral system laws are that a minimum of 10 per cent of votes have to be won by a party to be able to represent in parliament) winning 10.7 per cent of the votes and 61 seats. The HDP being pro-Kurdish has obvious sympathy for the PKK although they attempt to put forward a liberal narrative of peace. The violence blamed on the PKK has got the party stuck between Scylla and Charybdis and even some Kurdish supporters have abandoned them and returned to the AKP. The divisiveness of internal Kurdish politics is examined later. The main opposition party, Republican Peoples' Party (*Cumhuriyet Halk Partisi* or CHP) retained its June share of 25.4 per cent of the vote and 134 seats.

The AKP has declared the victory as an approval of its policies and more interestingly as a personal endorsement of Erdogan. The party now stays in power till 2019. The victory was crafted by adding a new challenge to the nation and then convincing the electorate that only AKP could solve it. The violence, which has been blamed completely on the PKK, will have to be contained fully almost immediately to ensure that the tactical political manoeuvring that has won the election for the AKP does not turn into a zero-sum game. The PKK cannot be subdued through military action.

Negotiations are the only way forward if the cycle of violence that engulfed the nation in the 1980s and 1990s are not to be repeated.

The election victory will not change Erdogan's general approach to politics and intolerance of criticism. If at all, the arrogance will only get entrenched. The fact is that any institution that could have enforced democratic norms and questioned the government policies have been effectively defanged in the past 13 years in a concerted manner, through the implementation carefully laid plans. The only development to watch out now is whether or not Erdogan will immediately pursue the plans to change the constitution and introduce a Presidential system of government. To alter the constitution the AKP needs the assistance of one of the other political parties, a simple majority in parliament is not sufficient to do so. Constitutional amendment to facilitate a presidential form of government has been a long term agenda and the priority laid in achieving it will tell the story of Erdogan's personal ambition.

Turkey's World View

Turkey's world view has always focused on the Middle-East and the AKP covets a significant role in the region and through it in the larger Islamic world. The AKP has pan-Islamic ambitions and wishes, rather craves, for a new regional order in which Turkey will play the most important role. Turkey wants to emphasise the allure of history while adhering to the concept of a nation-state with nationalism as an important cornerstone in the creation of such entities that it wants to share as a model with the rest of the Muslim world. In his attempt to recreate the Turkish state as a modern democratic republic, Mustafa Kemal Ataturk abandoned a centuries-old struggle for regional primacy and isolated Turkey in order to focus on nation-building. The new Turkey under the AKP and Erdogan invariably harks back to the lost glory of the Ottomans that it wants to regain and is therefore assiduously building a neo-Ottoman imperial agenda.

Turkey considers itself the natural leader of the Middle-East but also suffers from a sense of humiliation because of its failure to join or be accepted by the European Union (EU), which has been a steadfast aim of successive governments. A full integration with the West, Ataturk's glorious dream, is still unfulfilled. In order to understand some of the more incomprehensible actions that Turkey has recently initiated, they must be viewed through this complex prism of the national narrative.

The Turkey-Iran Equation

For centuries the Ottomans and the Persians, the only two non-Arb powers in the Middle-East, led rival empires for the domination of the region. Turkey and Iran, their contemporary successor states, have continued this millennium old rivalry and are today once again at cross purposes in the quest for the leadership of the broader Muslim world. However, in recent times they have shown some signs of willingness to reach an uneasy accommodation with each other. While open enmity is not visible, there is no overt friendship on display either—stand-off supporting the current status quo seems to be in place. Both the nations seem to be comfortable with functioning at the extreme grey area between aloofness and alliance. Turkey and Iran offer very different paths to regional stability; each based on the post-colonial experiences of the individual states. Over the past few decades the amorphous variations have coalesced into religious and ideological differences with both aspiring for wider recognition as regional powers. Whether this delicate situation will lead to a power sharing agreement is too far in the future to speculate upon.

Iran has its own ghosts to grapple with. It is still considered by the other regional states as a revolutionary state and Iran has an implicit belief that the regional balance of power is biased and tilted against it. If the region is stable, then Iran will be able to exert only minimal influence. However, when the region is in tumultuous instability and in the throes of sectarian violence, Iran can enhance its regional influence by supporting the groups that feel downtrodden, which creates a position of power for it within the Shiite world. Since the ultimate position of power is an eternal quest for both Iran and Turkey, Iran is not particularly enamoured with Erdogan's regional initiatives.

In spite of the mutual antipathy, Iran and Turkey share a broader and enduring economic relationship and there is an acceptance of the inter-dependence of the economies in both the nations. Even at the height of the sanctions in 2012-13, around 90 per cent of all Iranian gas was exported to Turkey. Turkey is the hub for oil and natural gas transfer, placed strategically between the suppliers and the customers. Iran is aware of this and of their dependence on the Turkish state for their energy export. Therefore, the competition between the two is carefully compartmentalised. The current conflict in Syria, where the two nations are placed on opposing ends of the spectrum however has the potential to rupture the carefully papered over divisions and ancient rivalries between the two neighbours.

The Kurdish Issue

It is often forgotten that the Kurds are the oldest inhabitants of Anatolia. Their demand for limited autonomy has created chronic unrest in Turkey since the 1980s, which tends to dominate the domestic agenda. After a brief respite in the past three years, the Kurdish issue has boiled over again. Sadly, when it comes to dealing with the Kurds, the ideals, rule of law and democracy all get pushed to the background by the mainstream Turks. The plight of the Turkish Kurds is unenviable. The pro-Kurdish HDP won 13.1 per cent of the votes in the June elections and called for peace at all costs. This is in direct contrast to the strategy adopted by the PKK, the traditional standard bearers of the Kurds, who were angered by this stance. Perhaps because of this rift, the PKK declared an end to the ceasefire that had been agreed with the government almost immediately after the HDP achieved their best-ever electoral result.

The PKK opposes civilian politics and within the party has legitimised the use of violence as a means to achieve their desired objectives. It is also aligned with the Syrian/Iraqi Kurds who are currently the only 'moderate' faction in the Syrian Civil War that has gained sufficient traction on the ground to be considered an influential group. Their latest victory in retaking the town of Sinjar from the Islamic State (IS) in Iraq underscores this point. The Syrian Kurds are aligned with the Western coalition and are being supplied and supported by the US. However, Turkey has steadfastly stuck to its stance of being against all and any Kurd group, irrespective of nationality.

The Kurdish issue has become a permanent feature in Turkey's political landscape. Ever since Mustafa Kemal founded the Republic, Kurdish identity has been suppressed by Ankara, often violently. As in many other nations with diverse ethnicities, the differences between the Kurds and Turks have been leveraged by politicians to advance their own selfish and often sectarian agendas. At the moment it seems that the differences between Turkish and Kurdish nationalism has reached an irreconcilable divide. Currently, street violence in Turkey is at an all-time high and the situation furthers an already inherent instability. The Turkish society is now divided into deeply mistrustful groups based on ethnicity and religious affiliations.

At the height of the Kurdish activities in the 1990s PKK had been declared a terrorist organisation by Turkey and the US. In the current and evolving political scenario in the region, PKK has aligned itself with Russia, Iran and what remains of the Assad regime in Damascus. The US has chosen to turn a Nelson's eye towards this emerging alliance. For the PKK what this means is that, for the first time they will be able to bring external influence to bear in their negotiations and dealings with Ankara. While the AKP's return to power will not change their attitude towards the Kurdish issue, they may not be able to contain it purely as a domestic issue anymore. Any future anti-Kurdish initiatives would be looked upon more closely by the greater powers with a vested interest in the region.

Turkey's Syrian Strategy

Under the AKP, Turkey has adopted an uncompromising stance, maintaining that only after the removal of the Assad regime would they participate in any negotiations regarding the future of Syria. The rigidity of this policy has created deep divisions in the nation's domestic politics, with the main opposition party CHP not being averse to negotiating with Assad. The AKP is unlikely to change its stance after the current re-election since there is no real incentive for them to change their Syria policy. However, the insistence on the removal of Assad as a pre-condition for peace efforts in Syria is an unrealistic objective in the current situation wherein Russia is actively supporting the regime and the Syrian Army.

The criticality of Syria to further Turkey's regional ambition is easier to understand if it is analysed taking into account the regional events of the past decade. On coming to power in 2002, Erdogan consciously ramped up Turkey's smart power in the Middle-East, improving Turkey's image and touting the AKP brand of 'democratic Islam' as a model. He was uniformly successful in this undertaking. By the time the so-called Arab Spring came about, Turkey, and particularly Erdogan, were at the height of their popularity in the region. Turkey's overarching reaction to the unfolding events was to sponsor Sunni Islamist groups wherever possible. This was severely criticised by other regional powers who accused Turkey of promoting extremism. In Egypt, Turkey's support for the Muslim Brotherhood failed and there is visible antagonism between Erdogan and the Egyptian President Abdel Fattah el-Sisi. Turkey also supports Hamas that had been declared a terrorist organisation by both the US and EU. In August, the Arab League passed a resolution condemning Turkey for bombing the PKK in northern Iraq. The fall from grace was rapid.

In 2011, when the Syrian civil war started, Turkey believed that Basher al-Assad would also go the Gadhafi way, and be removed quickly. This belief made Turkey support the hard-line factions in Syria, entering into and stoking the sectarian strife that was emerging. However, Turkey had not fully understood Assad's obstinate staying power and had miscalculated the regional dynamics. It had also underestimated the foreign support that Assad could rely upon—on hindsight it seems certain that Turkey had not factored the circling of the wagons by Iran, Hezbollah and Russia to provide pivotal military, political and economic support that continues to ensure Assad's regime survival. Turkey's inability to project power into the Syrian imbroglio is a sign of its waning influence in the region.

In the meantime, Assad has cleverly leveraged his country's geographical position to convert it into an energy corridor that would rival Turkey's attempt at doing the same thing by signing a $ 10 billion worth memorandum of understanding with Iran. The proposal is to create an 'Islamic pipeline' to carry natural gas from Iran towards its export market. This is a nuanced move that has long term implications for the economic developments in the region and abroad, which has not been sufficiently analysed or considered in the broader debate. Turkey could be left out in the cold.

Turkey has aligned its actions in Syria with Saudi Arabia in supporting Jabhat al-Nusra, the main Sunni, anti-Assad force other than the IS. This group has been credited with the territorial defeat of the Assad forces in early 2015, which was the catalyst for the Russian military intervention. The Russian actions were initially directed against the al-Nusra and other smaller groups fighting the Assad regime and both Turkey and Saudi Arabia were unable, and also unwilling, to do anything about this direct targeting of their allies and proxies. Turkey also has a military agreement with Qatar, and together they continue to sponsor the elements fighting the Assad regime. However, there is a clear understanding in both these nations that they would not commit ground forces in Syria.

Turkey currently is stuck with and committed to a strategy of regime change in Syria, although it has now become a failed initiative, with no meaningful effect on reality. It views with trepidation the rising influence and ambition of the Syrian Kurds, fearing that this would lead to an exacerbation of their own internal Kurdish issue. Therefore, in the political negotiations that are being initiated to find a solution to the Syrian Civil War, Turkey will vehemently oppose, and even veto if possible, any move towards providing even limited autonomy to the Syrian Kurds. Turkey is also mistrustful of US intentions in the region and this has become a core premise of all foreign policy development within Turkey. While Turkey is unwilling to accept it, the fact is clear that it is on a downward slope of decreasing relevance and influence. Turkey needs to rethink its foreign policy initiatives and align it more with international plans rather than continue to attempt to change the direction of the rest of the wider world community involved in the region.

Failing Foreign Policy

Turkey now faces a foreign policy crisis. Its Syrian policy has proven to be a mess; the relationship with Israel is strained almost to snapping point; Egypt and the UAE both oppose the concept of political Islam that Turkey ardently supports, thereby increasing tensions; Turkey considers Egyptian President al-Sisi unpalatable to deal with; and is at odds with Jordan for their tacit support for the Russian intervention. Russia is a now a major and critical player in the shifting geo-political order in the Middle-East, whether Turkey admits it or not. Turkey needs a more pragmatic and flexible approach to its foreign policy. The recent electoral victory and the four-year term that it entails should be used as an opportunity to take stock and alter core foreign policies to avoid the train wreck that is coming its way.

All the facts are pointing towards the need to revise its foreign policy. However, considering the past record of President Erdogan who calls all the shots in the ruling AKP, changes if any are instituted are bound to be biased and minimal. The AKP has repeatedly demonstrated an entrenched anti-Western sentiment and Erdogan has been abrasive in his anti-Western rhetoric. Given the corner that it has painted itself into, this is unlikely to be toned down in the near future. However, pragmatism dictates that with Iran now being part of the peace talks in Vienna, Turkey needs to reorient its foreign policy, if it is to continue to be relevant and influential in the region. While a U-turn may not be possible or palatable to the AKP and its leadership that is what it will take to regain lost traction.

The refugee crisis in Europe could provide an opening for Turkey to be seen to be proactive. Turkey does have an important role in resolving the crisis and Europe needs its cooperation. However, Turkey is likely to push a hard bargain and not look to creating good will. It will want a more liberalised visa regime for its citizens for entry into EU. Considering the recent events in Paris, this might not even be on the negotiating table. It is also unlikely that the refugee crisis and Turkey's cooperation in sorting it out will be sufficient to restart a push for EU Membership. After all the European nations are past masters at diplomatic negotiations and very good at compartmentalising different aspects of foreign policy.

In Conclusion…

Turkey has grandiose plans of creating a new 'global order', within which political Islam will find its rightful place. It believes that the regional autocracies in the Middle-East are doomed to failure and that they will be replaced by an elected government led by a 'man of the people'. The fact that such a person invariably turns out to be despotic and dictatorial, clinging to power long after his usefulness has become illusory, is lost in the hubris of this rhetoric. Turkey believes that it will be seen as the torchbearer in creating such a region which it would influence completely under the banner of pan-Islamism; the call to unite under Islam being the common denominator in this appeal. It is openly known that Islamist groups across the Middle-East are unofficial allies of the AKP and derive support from the party. In a single-focused pursuance of this agenda, the AKP has thrown aside the nation's much vaunted secularism with the convenient argument that secularism does not represent the will of the Turkish people. There is no evidence to prove this claim.

The AK-ruled Turkey today stands at a cross-road. The path it takes will determine Turkey's place in the global comity of nations into the future. If one is to hazard a guess—it would seem that at the end of the next four-year rule of the AKP, Turkey would be the hub of political Islam; and sectarian violence would have increased on the heels of religious intolerance. The painstakingly built 'Republic' of Mustafa Kemal may by then have been sacrificed to fulfil the biased, narrow-minded and sectarian ambition of a single individual.

Published in Eurasia Review 17 November 2015

http://www.eurasiareview.com/17112015-turkey-at-a-critical-juncture-analysis/

13

A METHOD TO MADNESS?
TURKEY SHOOTS DOWN A RUSSIAN
FIGHTER AIRCRAFT

On Tuesday 23 November a Russian Air Force Su-24 Fencer ground attack aircraft was shot down by an AIM-120 AMRAAM missile fired by a Turkish Air Force F-16 Fighting Falcon interceptor aircraft. The pilot was killed by ground fire after he and his navigator ejected successfully from the stricken aircraft and the navigator was later rescued by Syrian and Hezbollah commandos. The pilot was killed by ground fire from Turkmen militia with close links to Turkey. There is video evidence to prove that both the crewmen came under fire while they were descending in their parachutes, which is against the Geneva Convention and a war crime. Further, a Russian helicopter send to retrieve the Su-24 crew came under fire and was subsequently destroyed with the loss of one crew member. The attack on the helicopter was carried out by US-backed rebels with US-supplied TOW (Tube-launched Optically-tracked Wire-guided) missiles.

Ankara claims that it had warned the Russian fighter ten times before firing the missile because it threatened the security of the nation. However, it also accepts that the aircraft strayed into Turkish airspace only for a fleeting 17 seconds. It is difficult to imagine how a 17-second incursion by a single aircraft posed a security threat to Turkey. Following this incident, Russian President Vladimir Putin accused Turkey, and implicitly President Recep Tayyip Erdogan, of 'stabbing [Russia] in the back' and of being 'accomplices of terrorists'. Putin warned of serious consequences in the bilateral relationship between Russia and Turkey. The Russian Foreign

Minister Sergie Lavrov, cancelled his scheduled visit to Ankara, which was meant to improve this very relationship. During the initial war of words, the US kept a distance from the spat, denying any involvement in the fiasco.

Background

The shooting down of the Russian Su-24 cannot be viewed as an isolated incident—it has a long history behind it. On 22 June 2012, Syria shot down a Turkish F-4 Phantom Reconnaissance jet, almost certainly with a Russian supplied, and maybe even manned, air defence system. This increased the tension between Turkey and both Syria and Russia. Since then Turkey has been keen to demonstrate its capability to safeguard the sovereignty of its airspace. It had also managed to convince the US to deploy a Patriot air defence missile battery early this year in response to its concerns regarding air violations by Syrian aircraft. However, the battery is being withdrawn now, much against Turkey's wishes and 'demands' that they be left in place.

Politically, Erdogan has been vociferous in his condemnation of the Russian intervention in Syria, even warning that Turkey would re-examine the energy deal that it had agreed to with Russia. However, most observers considered it rhetorical bluster meant for a domestic audience. Turkey's position concerning Syria is at odds with that of Russia, especially with regard to the future of Basher al-Assad and his regime. The seven week old Russian campaign has wiped out all the 'gains' made by the US-Turkey-Saudi-Qatar supported jihadi terrorist groups. Currently the pro-Assad Syrian Army is on a winning streak with Russian support. This is anathema to Turkey, and the AKP's, read Erdogan's, electoral victory on 1 November seems to have increased its assertiveness and willingness to use military force. The shoot down of the fighter jet indicates a rigidity in Turkey's stance regarding Russia's expansion of its campaign.

Immediately on bringing the aircraft down, Turkey asked for an extraordinary meeting of NATO ambassadors. This was obviously a calculated move to—deter any immediate Russian military response; push for further US and NATO commitment to safeguarding the sovereignty of Turkey's airspace; and to throw a spanner on the French initiative for the 'Western' coalition to operate cooperatively with the Russian campaign against the Islamic State (IS) and other rebel groups, some of which are directly supported by Turkey. However, the European nations are unlikely to be swayed in support of Turkey since their domestic compulsions make them more interested in finding a political solution to the Syrian Civil War. Given the status of Turkey as a member of NATO, the incident is highly unlikely to be escalated into an air war, but there is no doubt that tensions between Russia and NATO will exacerbate.

Repercussions

This ill-considered action is akin to Turkey shooting itself in the foot and there will be immediate repercussions. Turkey has been pushing strongly to create what it calls a 'safe zone' along its southern borders, but in Syrian territory. This safe zone, in actuality a no-fly zone, is meant to provide sanctuary for the extremist Turkmen that it supports and who act as Turkey's foot soldiers in its bid to remove Assad from power and convert Syria into a Turkish vassal state. The act of toppling the Assad regime is the centrepiece in realising Erdogan's dream of creating a new 'Caliphate' with Turkey as the core. After the November election victory, the AKP has been concentrating on salvaging and reinstating a failed strategy that aims to replace a secular Syrian government with an Islamic one. With this single aerial encounter the concept of a 'safe zone', from within which the Turkmen would operate into Syria to remove Basher al-Assad, has died a premature death even before seeing the light of day.

So who are these Turkmen? They inhabit the Latakia region of Syria and are reported to have numbered more than 200,000 before the Civil War. They are allied with Turkey and are Sunni Muslims speaking a language that is very close to Turkish. They have always maintained intimate relations with the Turks, because of ethnic and linguistic closeness, so much so that Turkey considers the Turkmen region its historical legacy inside Syria. At the start of the Syrian Civil War, the Turkmen formed a rebel group with active Turkish assistance and was one element of the militia called the Free Syrian Army.

Turkey had struggled to sell the idea of a 'safe zone' to NATO for three reasons. First, the affiliation of the Turkish-backed rebel groups who would have occupied these areas was uncertain and second, their ability to clear the IS on the ground from these areas was also seen to be at best questionable. The third reason, perhaps more important that the other two, is that the creation of a safe zone would have brought NATO into direct confrontation with Russia's strategic objective of securing the Assad regime, since Russia would have retaliated against the Turkish-backed rebel groups who would have inhabited the area. In these circumstances, downing the Russian fighter aircraft could also be seen as an action meant to nudge or incite NATO to confront Russia directly. What is certain, however, is that by opting to openly display its chauvinistic nationalism, Turkey has once and for all let the chances of enforcing its concept of the creation of a safe/no-fly zone go up in smoke. In any case, the viability of the concept had always been in question.

The Existing Dichotomies

The only nation that is operating legally within sovereign Syrian airspace or on the ground is Russia, since it was invited by the government of the nation to intervene. Irrespective of the 'feeling' of nations like Turkey or Saudi Arabia, and even the US, and their argument that the Assad regime has lost its legitimacy, the fact remains that it is the legal government of Syria. The US and its allies are therefore carrying out attacks in Syrian territory in direct violation of existing international law. The attack on Russian military forces by Turkey, for that is what shooting down the Su-24 clearly denotes, makes the US only one step removed from the unlawful action—irrespective of the declaration of their non-involvement. The US is being drawn deeper into the conflict, with or without its consent.

Turkey has violated Syrian airspace many times and attacked targets within Syria without the permission of the Syrian Government. Its ground forces have conducted operations within Syrian territory and Turkey provides direct support to armed groups that want to overthrow the legitimate Syrian regime. Irrespective of Turkey's liking or otherwise for the current Assad regime in Syria, all these acts are illegal and is condemnable within international norms. Yet Turkey opted to attack the only armed force operating legally in Syria. Had it not been for the seriousness of the situations, the dichotomy would have been almost funny.

Conjectures

There are two ways of looking at Turkey's maverick actions. First is that the actions obviously had at least the tacit approval of the US, even though they are now distancing themselves from the fall-out. If this is indeed the case, it is believable that Ankara may have been asked to take this step to stop, or at least slow down, the increasing influence that Russia has started to wield in the region. With Russian assistance, the Assad regime has started to flex its military muscle and is gradually changing from an almost defeated entity to having a fighting chance at keeping the rebels at bay indefinitely. This is not palatable to some in the US coalition, especially Turkey and the Arab block.

Second is a more sinister situation, where Turkey has blind-sided the US and NATO with this action, where it will be able to evoke the 'mutual assistance' clause to make these nations come to its aid, as and when Russia retaliates. If this is the case, there are a number of underlying reasons for Turkey to have initiated this action. The Paris attacks have changed the Western perception regarding Turkey's insistent claim that its jihadi Turkmen would be able to gain the upper hand and rule Syria. By claiming that it has acted in self-defence Turkey is creating a false impression to bring in NATO, and by default the US, deeper into the conflict and may be even draw them into a ground war. Only a ground intervention would give the Turkmen rebels, Turkey's foot soldiers, a reasonable chance of making some gains against the Syrian regime. Turkey has depicted the Russian air violation as a threat to its security as a reason for the downing of the Su-24, an explanation that hangs on a slender thread in terms of authenticity.

The effectiveness of the Russian intervention made the AKP leadership realise that their strategy of using the Civil War to expand Turkey's geo-political reach meant to cater to their neo-Ottoman fantasies was rapidly failing. Something had to be done to bring the strategy and the dream back on track. Russia's restrained response to the episode, at least from a military perspective, has once again thwarted the initiative. Turkey is in a far more precarious condition now than before the unfortunate incident.

President Putin knows fully well that he needs to respond, strongly and decisively. His long-term aim is to restore Russia as a global power as the natural successor and with the same status as the erstwhile Soviet Union. It is likely that Russia believes that the action is a push-back to its growing regional influence being orchestrated by the US, using Turkey as a pawn. However, the US may not be able to cajole the rest of NATO into becoming more belligerent and initiating actions against Russia, more than the sanctions that have already been put in place. The European nations know that in the case of a war, the geographic battlefield will once again be their own backyards. More importantly, they are already war-weary and domestic issues that have to be surmounted are gradually taking precedence over foreign military adventures. There is a ground swell of anti-American sentiment in Europe that could become further entrenched if the US pushes too hard for action. Putin senses this clearly.

Within a week of the shooting down, the incident has already forced all participants to reconsider their individual positions in both the Syrian Civil War and the broader fight against the IS. This incident has all the hallmarks of becoming the most important game changer in the long-running Syrian conflict and could define the future of Russia's relationship with the West. There is a high likelihood of Russia swinging back to full support for Basher al-Assad and an acknowledged partnership with Iran. The earlier and more flexible stance, where it was tacitly understood that Assad would only play a temporary role leading to his eventual removal, would now be off the negotiating table. The pendulum has swung fully to the other side.

The current impasse is also turning out to be a critical test for NATO's commitment to its members. As yet there has not been unequivocal support for Turkey and its intransigence is being viewed with scepticism. The Baltic States are already wary of NATO's commitment to their security in the face of Russian belligerence and may not be forthcoming in supporting actions to protect Turkey. Another factor that must be closely monitored is NATO reaction to Turkey's continuing dealings with the IS; its gradually declining adherence to human rights; the muzzling of the press; and the spreading religious intolerance in the country. NATO's actions in the coming weeks will determine the future of the alliance.

Russia's Options

Russia had a number of options available to it at the start of the stand-off. The first was to immediately mount a retaliatory attack on Turkey's bases. Very prudently they avoided this course of action, which would have led to escalation and a possible Russia-West conflict coming to a head. The US operates from some of Turkey's air bases and would have been caught in the middle of a Russia-Turkey conflict. Further, a direct Russian attack would have made it easy for Turkey to evoke Article 5—the mutual protection clause—of the NATO alliance. Currently, even with claims of national security being jeopardised by the incursion of the Russian fighter, Turkey is finding it hard to evoke the clause since the claim is extremely tenuous. There is however, a distinct possibility that the Russian Air Force operating in Syria would shoot down any Turkish aircraft that violates Syrian airspace. It is certain that the Russian detachment in Syria would be operating under revised rules of engagement.

The second option, some parts of which have been already put in place, is economic and trade sanctions that Russia can evoke against Turkey. Russia is Turkey's second largest trading partner and supplies more than half of Turkey's natural gas imports, which has now been put within the sanctions. Russia has in the past few days—stopped imports from Turkey; stopped visa-free travel for Turkish citizens; asked for the repatriation of all Turkish citizens currently in Russia, estimated to be 90,000 strong, working in Russian companies; and ended all charter flights between the nations. The construction of the Akkuyu nuclear plant is also on the line to be halted.

The third option, which could also be gradually introduced is to provide direct aid to both Syrian and Turkish Kurds and also provide air cover for their operations if necessary. Such a move would have the added advantage of tying up the Turkish military indefinitely in a war of attrition that could progressively strain the Turkish economy. The fourth option is for Russia to become even more involved in Ukraine through ramping up support for the breakaway provinces of Donetsk and Lugansk. This would be logical since Ukraine and Russia share centuries of history, more as one country than two. In an indirect manner, Russia could demonstrate its chagrin to the European nations.

The fundamental fact is that Putin cannot but demonstrate strength at this juncture, especially with Erdogan's highly confrontational pronouncements even if they were meant for domestic consumption. There is a feeling among observers that this time Erdogan's rhetoric and actions went far beyond what were necessary. Russia's Syrian expedition has so far been strategically good for the country, bringing it back into global relevance and Putin will not let Turkey spoil it. The stakes in the Syrian conflict, for all participants, just went up one big notch.

Conclusion

By a thoughtless action, Turkey has strengthened the jihadi cause. However, considering its proclivity for siding with the Syrian rebels, this could very well have been a calculated act that has backfired. The result is that it has become a hundred-fold more difficult to find a solution to the Syrian crisis that is spiralling out of control. In four and one half years that it has been raging, the Civil War has led to the death of unaccounted thousands and to the rise of the IS. These are facts that seem lost on Turkey's leadership who are single-mindedly obsessed with the removal of the Assad regime. Pursuing this aim in a blinkered manner, Turkey did not close its borders with Syria, becoming the transit point for IS sympathisers to join its ranks and in the bargain making Syria the haven of global jihadists.

Turkey blames Russia for attacking the Turkmen and other anti-Assad groups while itself carrying out air attacks against the Kurds who are at the forefront of the fight against the IS. The immediate question that emerges is whether or not Turkey is serious about fighting the IS or waiting in the wings to create a grand geo-political alliance with the IS to create its cherished 'Caliphate'. Trying to precipitate a crisis by shooting down a Russian fighter aircraft somehow reinforces the belief that Turkey's leadership has prioritised warped objectives for the nation.

For the Western coalition, the crisis marks a moment of decision. It has to choose between continuing an almost unwinnable fight against the IS or accepting the Basher al-Assad regime till a relatively peaceful transfer of power can be affected at some future date. With the Arab lobby and Turkey at odds with this option, it is hard to predict where subsequent events will lead, although it is certain that the world is witnessing the beginning of an upheaval much larger and more eventful than before. Putin cannot afford to let the event go unpunished and the enforcement of sanctions that have been announced will only be the first of many actions that is bound to follow. He is unlikely to let the rest of the world forget that Russia is the only country acting legitimately in Syria. Turkey has strategically isolated itself, at least for the moment, through the maverick actions of its ego-centric and narrow focused leadership

Published in Eurasia Review 2 December 2015

http://www.eurasiareview.com/02122015-a-method-to-madness-turkey-shoots-down-russian-fighter-aircraft-analysis/

14

THE MIDDLE-EAST
AN OPEN PANDORA'S BOX

Even before the discovery of the vast oil reserves in the region, the Middle-East had been the stomping ground of the global powers of the time. The past century has seen the region embroiled in convoluted conflicts that have simmered and altered shape, but have never really been brought to a complete or desirable conclusion. However, in the past few decades the situation has become incomprehensible with fundamentalist Islamic extremism increasingly engulfing every aspect of life for the people of the region, which has now become the centrepiece in global politico-economic and security considerations. Since the outbreak of the Syrian Civil War in 2011, international attention has been focused on the manoeuvrings of global powers in the region. Adding to this political confusion is the inherent religious and sectarian divide that has plagued the region for centuries. The Middle-East is the powder keg that could blow the world apart.

The region has given rise to the most violent jihadist movement that the world has yet seen in the form of the Islamic State (IS). The reasons for its rise and how it can be defeated are vexed issues that defy answers and the debate on both counts is on-going. It will be of interest to analyse the objectives of the different nations involved in the regional war and understand the reasons for the prioritisation of these objectives by the respective countries. The participants in the melee are many and cannot easily be placed even within broad groupings—the US-led coalition consisting of NATO and other Western nations; the regional nations, some functioning within the US coalition and some outside; Russia, Iran and the Hezbollah; the legal government of Syria; the rebel groups fighting to oust the Syrian regime; IS, Jabhat al-Nusra and a horde of other Islamic extremist groups; and the Kurds. The interaction between these nations, groups and jihadists are complex and not always openly visible. There are wheels within wheels rotating in the Middle-East and the Pandora's Box is open.

The United States and its Western Allies

The US has been involved in some manner or the other in the Middle-East from the end of World War II and through the long trek of decolonisation in the region that followed. Even though the US intervened militarily in 1991 to liberate Kuwait from Saddam Hussein, the invasion of Iraq in 2003 was the one single event that changed the complexion of the Middle-East, ushering in unmitigated chaos. Almost all the developments of the past 15-odd years can be traced back to that ill-advised and ill-conceived military action.

When the Civil War started in Syria as a movement to oust the Basher al-Assad regime, the US was quick to support the rebels. It wanted to effect a regime change in Syria but at the same time also avoid another Iraq and Libya, nations that are still reeling under the consequences of US-instituted regime changes. Four and one half years into the Syrian Civil War, the conflict is without doubt or exaggeration, a bigger mess than anything witnessed before—no one clearly knows who is fighting whom and why; there is no differentiation between the 'good' guys and the 'bad' guys, since perceptions vary with the view of the beholder; half the population of the country is either dead or displaced; the nation has' no civilian infrastructure to speak off; the Assad regime is holed up in Damascus and continuing to kill its own people; and the US is hated as never before, both within Syria and in the broader region. If this is not a mess, what is?

For the US and its allies, the lack of direct approval by the United Nations and the questionable legality within International Law for their intervention are becoming increasingly awkward issues to explain away. At the same time 'victory' in the conflict, however it is defined, is receding into the horizon. In this situation, where the definition of victory is amorphous, mission creep is setting in and the US is deploying more Special Forces to partner with Iraqi forces, the Free Syrian Army and the Kurdish fighters. Once again, the ultimate military objective of this deployment remains obscure.

The US is also embroiled in the region's power play between the Sunni Muslim Arab monarchies and the Shiite, non-Arab Iran. At the fundamental level Saudi Arabia and the Persian Gulf monarchies have two points of commonality—they are vociferously opposed to Assad continuing as the legitimate ruler of Syria; and they will not willingly cede even an iota of influence to Iran. These nations continue to be part of the US-led coalition, at least on paper, although they have been 'missing in action' for the past few months. Apart from the military actions, the US is negotiating a tortuous path in Middle-Eastern politics. It now appreciates that only a negotiated settlement in Syria can bring some semblance of stability to the region. Towards this end it has taken two steps. First it has softened its position regarding the removal of Assad, and second it has tacitly accepted that without the participation of Iran, there can be no viable negotiation. Both these issues are sticking points for the Arab nations—they do not want Iran to participate in any peace deal and they want Assad to step down as a precondition to commence negotiations. The fact remains that there is no possibility of arriving at a negotiated peace without the active involvement of Iran, however much Saudi Arabia and its Sunni Muslim Arab allies hate it.

In the recent past both the British and German parliaments have voted in support of initiating military action against the IS in Syria and Iraq. This may not significantly increase the coalition capabilities in terms of the quantum of military weight that can be brought to bear, but the political and moral factors indicate a strong current against the IS in Western democracies as well as the willingness to fight a common threat. Further, even though there is no UN sanction for the military action, by increasing international participation it bolsters the legitimacy of the intervention. For the Western coalition destruction on IS is the highest priority objective. France's President Francois Hollande has been doing the diplomatic rounds in an effort to create a grand coalition that would include Russia to confront and defeat global terrorism. However, the effort has not borne any fruit so far, the political and ideological gap between Russia and the West and the differences in their strategic objectives are far too broad to be filled easily.

Saudi Arabia

Pragmatism regarding issues of religion and the concept of religious tolerance has never been Saudi Arabia's strong suite. Their rigid sectarian stance on matters of religion and blind support for, and propagation of, the puritanically extreme version of Salafist Wahabi Islam has gradually changed the Western nations' attitude to Saudi Arabia. The genesis of IS can be traced to years of Saudi support for the proliferation of this particularly virulent form of Islam. The Western nations, so far complacent about Saudi Arabian activities in the religious sphere, have started to wake up to the reality of the menace being created. Now there a visible, although subtle, shifts in policy; clear statements by senior politicians for Saudi Arabia to change course; and directly hostile articles in mainstream media accusing Saudi Arabia of fomenting religious extremism and jihadist attacks. This loss of political influence is accompanied by a weakening of Saudi economic influence in the wake of the drop in oil prices.

Even so, Saudi Arabia is still being handled with kid-gloves by the Western governments, for two reasons. One, Saudi Arabia is a crucial market for Western arms sales—just in the last 18 months the US approved the sale of $24 billion worth of weaponry to the kingdom. Two, and a critical reason for the reluctant support to the Saudi monarchy, is that it is a fact of life in the Middle-East that when one bad regime falls or is removed, it is invariably replaced by a worse regime. In the case of Saudi Arabia the main opponents to the monarchy are not liberal democrats, but hard-line Islamists. The fall of the House of Saud will be accompanied by the chaos of a failed state that the world can ill-afford at this juncture.

While this consideration does hold back definitive action against Saudi Arabia, results in reigning back the desert kingdom will only be achieved if the gloves are removed. This may be a hard act to carryout, since the West needs to work collaboratively with Saudi Arabia to curtail their on-going support to global jihadists. A first step would be to insist that religious tolerance be practised by Saudi Arabia in a similar manner to their asking for such tolerance in other countries. The double standards that the Saudis have practised for decades, where they go around building mosques and propagating a particularly reprehensive form of Islam around the world while denying any other religion even a place of worship within the kingdom, has to stop. The liberal democratic world must now insist that the religious freedom that the Islamic faith expects in all parts of the world must also be reciprocated in Saudi Arabia. The other option will be to curtail and stop Islamic activities in other parts of the world. The fundamental Wahabi strain of Islam cannot be allowed to spread any more than it already has in the world, thanks to Saudi Arabia. This will be a first step in bringing Saudi Arabia in line with 'normal' nations.

Turkey

Turkey has so far played an ambiguous but definitely self-centred role in the developing imbroglio although it is a reluctant and late-entry member of the US-led coalition. Turkey can be considered at par with Saudi Arabia as a terrorist support centre and the Islamic zealotry of the ruling party can no longer be hidden under the platitudes of its leadership. It is also focused single-mindedly on ensuring that the Syrian Kurds do not prevail in obtaining autonomy so that their own long subjugated Kurdish citizens will not aspire to something similar. Turkey is also paranoid regarding the increasing regional influence of Iran and Russia, while its commitment to fighting violent jihadism is questionable. Its 'impulsive' actions have complicated matters in the region—the shooting down of the Russian fighter aircraft, and more recently the deployment of a 400-strong Commando battalion into Iraq on 4 December 2015 carry the hallmark of a maverick.

Turkey's hypocrisy was demonstrated with the shooting down of the Russian fighter aircraft that had violated its sovereign airspace for a mere 17 seconds by its own admission. Compare this to the report that Turkey has been responsible for 2000 air violations into Greek airspace in 2014 alone! In these circumstances, NATO nations must consider a future situation where Turkey will initiate precipitate action, possibly against Russia, which will not be as restrained in its response as it was during the Su-24 incident in late November. The dire consequences of Turkey being a NATO member is becoming amply clear to other nations. The NATO alliance is one of peaceful democracies and at least for the time being, Turkey is neither. It is not at peace with any of its neighbours and it can at best be described as an 'illiberal democracy' which does not afford protection to any dissent.

Turkey also wants the immediate removal of the Basher al-Assad regime and the establishment of a 'safe zone' in Syrian territory. This is a euphemism to steal Syrian territory and protect its proxy warriors, the Turkmen, in that region. Regime change in Syria is one of the fundamental objectives of the US-led coalition and of Turkey itself. The difference is that the US wants to remove Assad after defeating the IS, whereas Turkey wants it done irrespective of the status of the IS. The dichotomy in priorities is clearly visible. There is also divergence between the so-called allies in their dealings with the Kurds. Turkey is fighting their own Kurdish population represented by the PKK, a group that espouses violence to gain independence. The US supplies and supports the Syrian Kurds—aligned with the Turkish PKK—as the only element on the ground in Syria with any noticeable traction in the conflict. Allies at cross purposes.

Despite their recalcitrant attitude and the differences of opinion regarding Syria, the Turkish leadership was able to strike a politico-economic deal with members of the European Union to stop the flow of immigrants to Europe. This deal displayed on world stage the shallowness of 'political integrity' and the fact that the term itself was an oxymoron. Turkey will continue to look after its narrow and sectarian interests and will muddy the waters when events that are not conducive to its perceived interests take place. Perhaps it is time for NATO to take good hard look at the pros and cons of continuing to have Turkey within the alliance, if the ultimate objective is to further world peace.

Russia has accused Turkey, and President Erdogan personally, of profiting from the oil trade with the IS. It is a known fact that bulk of the IS oil is exported through conduits in Turkey. It is now time for NATO and Europe to ensure that Turkey abandons its diplomatic ambiguity and targets the IS funding mechanism, based on oil trade carried out through Turkish territories. This is a critical step that has to be taken at the earliest, if the defeat of IS is actually a strategic objective.

Russia

The Russian intervention has without doubt created some effects and elicited reactions from the Western coalition. However, for Russia the campaign continues to be a risky gamble, primarily because the infrastructure necessary to mount a successful air campaign is lacking in Syria and is still to be built up. The Russian agenda in Syria is to regain the status of an influential regional player that was lost to Russia at the breakup of the Soviet Union and to protect the Basher al-Assad regime. Within this two-pronged initiative, the defeat of IS is only a sub-set of the broader strategy. It is more important for Russia at this juncture in the Syrian Civil War to defeat the rebel groups who are directly opposing the Assad regime. President Barak Obama has called for Russia to choose the welfare of the Syrian State rather than the Assad regime. However, from a Russian perspective, it is far too early in the intervention to make this call.

The call by the French President to create a grand coalition is similar to the overtures that President Putin had made in the early stages of the intervention. However, the deteriorating Russia-Turkey relationship, has been a step backward and could become a show stopper in bettering relations with the West. There is also the difficulty in aligning the strategic objectives of the US and Russia— defeat of IS is the first priority for the US, whereas protecting the Assad regime is the priority for Russia. Russia has also proposed creating clear spheres of influence akin to what existed in the post-World War II decades. Some of the European nations have indicated that they are not averse to examining this proposal. What is to be watched is the kind of balance between advantages that cooperation with Russia will bring and the price that the Western nations are willing to pay for it. In this equation the future of Ukraine is being left unsaid. There is a belief in some quarters that the military intervention in Syria was a Russian ploy to divert the spotlight from Ukraine. This is incorrect, Russia is only protecting its national interests by the employment of its military forces in Syria. Any chance of the West and Russia working together to defeat the IS will depend entirely on the West's ability to delink Ukraine and Syria in their dealings with Russia.

There is a perception in the Western media that Russia is 'returning' to the Middle-East. This is wrong. Yes, there was a loss of status as mentioned earlier, but Russia had never 'left' the region. Syria was a steadfast Soviet ally during the entire Cold War and Russia is only standing by an old and trusted friend. In stark contrast to the US abandoning Mubarak in Egypt, under less stressful conditions, by standing by the Assad regime in extremely difficult circumstances Russia is demonstrating its commitment to its 'friends' for the Middle-Eastern leadership to see. Moral of the story—Russia can be trusted and is loyal to its friends without any hidden caveats. Russia has been engaging with the Middle-Eastern nations and the continuing dialogues strengthens its strategic stance in the region. There are two sub-sets of the intervention that is often overlooked. One, Russia has shown that it not averse to taking bold, decisive, and difficult decisions; and two, it has proven the sceptics, who had written off the Russian military as incompetent, completely wrong.

Russia, amongst all the external intervening powers, seems to understand best that the collapse of the Assad regime will mean the beginning of a far greater and messier conflict and the establishment of another Libya-like situation, not peace and stability to the region. Syria is Russia's long term strategic investment in the Middle-East, starting from the 1950s. While it protects the Assad regime, Russia has indicated that it is not particularly beholden to Basher al-Assad or worried about the future leadership that will emerge in a negotiated settlement as long as its strategic interests in the region are protected. This is pragmatic real politic at its best.

After one of its fighter jets was shot down by Turkey, Russian reaction was measured. While enforcing economic and political sanctions it has embarked on a single-minded campaign to isolate Turkey from the West. It has asked the UN Security Council to discuss Turkey's involvement in the military operations in Syria and Iraq and unleashed a barrage of propaganda regarding Turkey's dubious oil trade. Turkey is clearly in the crosshairs of the Russian rifle.

Iran

The future of Syria is a core national interest for Iran—it is the only route for Iran's materiel support to reach the Hezbollah; and Syria is home to a number of Shiite religious sites that are important for Iran. The religious angle is a factor that is not often considered or articulated. It is obvious that Iran cannot afford to have a hostile Sunni government ruling Syria. Even a change of leadership from Basher al-Assad carries too high a risk for Iranian strategic interests. Focusing on this key objective, Iran has developed a modus operandi that has so far been successful. It has created a powerful Shiite militia that is loyal to Iran and more powerful than the traditional Syrian Army. This force has been successful in keeping the rebel forces at bay from the core areas around Damascus for more than four years. In case required, this force will be able to replace the Syrian government.

Iran wants a future Syria that continues to maintain an anti-Israeli stance and continues to be a conduit for support to Hezbollah in Lebanon. This is the primary reason why Iran cannot, and will not, compromise with the US-led coalition regarding Syria's political future. Iran shares with Russia a commonality in the envisaged short-term future of Syria, although the approach to achieve this is distinctly different. Russia has made some sort of a deal with Israel, for the short-term and Iran is out of that equation. However, the long term future that Iran and Russia would like for Syria is completely divergent from each other and there are no chances of them ever merging. For Iran, the Syrian Government has to remain a Shiite entity, whereas for Russia the religious inclination is immaterial as long as it continues to wield the same strategic influence in the country.

Fighting the IS – Defining Victory

Victory in war is defined contextually and encompasses all power projection capabilities of a nation. The military is only a small but critical part of the whole. Even military victory is perceived in different ways by the participants. In the fight against the IS, the current state of affairs is such that only the military aspects of the conflict are being addressed although it constitutes only a small part of the larger picture. There is a visible reluctance amongst the liberal democracies to question the Islamic ideology in the conflict with the IS. In some cases, such as this, ideological confrontation is the best way forward to ensure victory. Such a stance by the secular democratic nations of the world could also act as an impetus for the Muslims of the world to reject the questionable religious ideology that is being propagated by the IS as the one and only 'true' interpretation of the Islamic faith.

There is enough historical evidence to support the idea that the IS cannot be defeated purely through military means. Obviously the first step to obtain a military victory against the IS is to seize the offensive from it. This can only be achieved by land operations that disrupt the ability of the IS to communicate and conduct operations at will. Air power is dominant in the region now and disruption can be effected by Special Forces functioning behind and around the IS strongholds. Simultaneously, initiatives have to be put in place to making the popular support for IS vanish. What would this involve, especially when both Turkey and Saudi Arabia continue to indirectly support IS activities? The offensive on this front has to be three-pronged: deprive IS of its ability to sell oil and create finances to support itself, gradually starving it of resources; target its ability to provide basic civil services to the people in the territories that it controls, which might involve neutralising purely civilian facilities; mount an ideological campaign against the violent Islamism being advocated by the IS.

The counter offensive against IS religious propaganda is a prerequisite for any of the other initiatives are to succeed. Perceived political correctness that stops mentioning Islam in discussions of terrorism is as bad as blaming all Muslims for terrorist attacks. Secular democratic leaders have to carefully, but strongly, articulate that Islamist extremism is behind acts of terrorism and human rights abuses across the world, a fact that most 'moderate' Western

Muslims tend to deny. This head in the sand attitude has to confronted and set right through a concerted effort. If this changed strategy is to work, the Sunni Arab nations of the Middle-East will have to look beyond the here and now and accept that Basher al-Assad and Iran are not the ultimate enemies to their well-being, but that the IS is. Only a comprehensive defeat of the IS will pave the first step towards stability in the region.

The Future of the Military Campaign

Currently there are two distinct coalitions operating within Syria and Iraq—the US-led coalition of NATO and some Arab monarchies, and the Russia-Iran combine. The ease of understanding the situation on the ground ends with the above statement. The IS is the fundamental and most powerful adversary that is being fought by the US-led coalition, at least officially. There are a number of other rebel and Islamist groups in the conflict that are supported by some of the coalition members while some others target the same groups. Jaish al-Fath, which consists of Jabhat al-Nusra an al-Qaeda affiliate and Harkat Ahrat al-Sham, is the next powerful grouping supported politically and materially by both Saudi Arabia and Turkey. The difference between IS and this group is only in the level of violence and barbarity that they perpetuate. At least for the moment, Russia seems to have distinguished between IS and Jaish al-Fath and also clearly sees the danger of either of them coming to power in Syria.

The military campaign in the Middle-East lacks a coherent and overarching strategy, is completely uncoordinated, and has some elements within the Western coalition supporting rebel groups with unsupportable objectives. The two opposing coalitions will have to work together if a military victory is to be achieved. Although there are a number of difficulties in creating such an alliance, they are certainly not insurmountable or irreconcilable if there is the political will to do so. The stumbling blocks will be the nations contributing the least to the military effort against the IS at the moment, Turkey and Saudi Arabia.

A recent and interesting development has been the Syrian Government's declaration that no further violation of its airspace will be tolerated. The Russian forces have deployed highly capable S-300 and S-400 air defence systems in the more volatile areas and therefore this declaration has to be taken seriously. When it is clear that the US-led coalition is operating within Syrian airspace illegally, the any further action ensuing from this warning will have to be considered show stoppers. Immediately after the shooting down of the Russian fighter aircraft by a Turkish jet, the US President had supported the action by releasing the statement that Turkey had the right to defend its airspace. If Syria opts to act on its warning, the same logic can be applied to defending its airspace also; the chicken has come home to roost rather fast! Only the Russian military is operating in Syria legally.

The Future of Syria – A Notion of Peace

In the frenzy of fighting the IS and other assorted groups creating chaos in Iraq and Syria, none of the intervening powers have even attempted to articulate a vision of the future for Syria. At least for the moment the only discussion taking place is regarding the future of the Assad regime. The Civil War in Syria, which started as a rebellion against the current Government more than four years back, has now become a conflict of multiple inter-locking layers. There is disagreement within the coalitions, disputes within the anti-Assad rebels, and even between different Islamist jihadists. Enveloping this scenario is the region-wide conflict between Sunnis and Shias.

What kind of a Syria will emerge from this mess, if one emerges at all? There are few certainties that can be listed. First, a return to its original borders as a cohesive country will be impossible. Second, there cannot be a strong successor government to the Assad regime since there are no mechanisms that exist to support such a government. Third, there can be no peace in Syria till Russia and Iran are brought into the circle of negotiations. Working against their intentions is unlikely to succeed even in the long term. Fourth, if and when a negotiated settlement takes place and a post-Assad political process is initiated, the IS with its virulent ideology can never be part of that process. Fifth, the current Turkish leadership will never permit autonomy for the Syrian Kurds for fear of the concept spreading to their own Kurds.

At the end of the Civil War, Syria can only emerge as a confederation with a weak central authority that ties together various autonomous sectors ruled by separate individual institutions. This is perhaps the only way forward to avoid complete disintegration that will in turn usher in greater chaos and anarchy than existing now. Even this situation will be unachievable if Turkey and the PKK both do not exhibit at least a modicum of flexibility, since one of the autonomous regions in Syria will have to be controlled by the Syrian Kurds. Any semblance of stability in the region hinges on the possibility of creating the atmosphere to put in place a workable confederation.

Basher al-Assad's streak of stubbornness and his intransigent nature that has so far made him refuse to heed calls for his resignation will also be a factor that will slow the negotiations when they take place. Saudi Arabia has convened a conference of various Syrian rebel groups to iron out their differences and create a coherent opposition. There seems to have been some success in this attempt. However, given the sectarian interests at play, it is too early to consider it even a glimmer of hope.

Conclusion

Since the invasion of Afghanistan in 2001, the world has been witnessing an erosion in the traditional concept of sovereignty, mainly because of the US-led Western military interventions, especially in the Middle-East. These forces have carried out proxy wars supported by concerted media campaigns that have led to illegal regime changes in designated 'rogue' enemy states. By the actions that have been initiated by the US and its allies from the beginning of the 21st century, a perception has been gradually built-up that the Western nations take military action, even without UN sanctions, against regimes that are inflexible to their demands and obdurate in their dealings with the West. In the current situation there is a feeling also percolating that the air strikes are being carried out to cover up Western and Turkish collusion with some of the terrorist groups. In the Syrian Civil War the US claim that they are fighting the IS to defeat them is viewed sceptically since there seems to be a lack of immediacy and commitment to stabilising the region. Clearly this is a case of too little too late.

A start has been made to negotiate the way forward in Syria to end the conflict and then solve the issue of governance. The International Syria Support Group, which consists of all the nations involved in the conflict, has announced the convening of a meeting on 1 January 2016 of the Syrian Government and opposition representatives under the auspices of the UN. This move could, if successful, be a step forward to bridge the gap between the Western coalition and Russia. However, Iran continues to be an enigma in all these moves.

Within a broad analysis it is clear that an end to combat activities in the current Civil War is a long way away for a large number of reasons.

One: there are far too many warring factions with varying ideologies and motivation on the ground that will hamper the chances of the rebels creating a unified negotiating position. Two: the opposition is far too fractured to be able to come to an agreement in giving the lead representation to a single group in the negotiation process. Three: the Kurds, especially the PKK in Turkey, will push for increased and guaranteed autonomy that will not be forthcoming, which in turn will act as a catalyst for continuing the conflict. Four: even if hypothetically it is accepted that all rebel groups, the Government and the intervening nations lay down arms, the IS and Jabhat al-Nusra will continue to exist and take violent action to further their interests. Five: the external interventionists are divided regarding whom to attack and whom to support, both morally and materially. Six: putting an end to support for belligerent rebel groups will be a complicated process and highly unlikely to succeed because of the differing objectives and priorities of the nations that make up the Western coalition. Each nation will continue to support their own proxies, all of whom claim to be fighting the IS and Jabhat al-Nusra, and will want their favourite group to have an advantage at the negotiating table. Seven: there is no unanimous agreement on the future of Basher al-Assad, with different views being expressed for the short term and no convincing position being articulated for the period after a transition of power takes place.

Currently two groups of nations with almost diametrically opposed objectives are involved in military actions in Syria over which the legitimate Syrian Government has no control. The future of the nation, if it continues to exist as one, is at best bleak. The obstacles to reaching a reasonable settlement point are so many that such a situation is not even a speck in the far horizon in Syria. An extremely sad but true statement.

Published in Eurasia Review 13 December 2015

http://www.eurasiareview.com/13122015-the-middle-east-an-open-pandoras-box-analysis/

CONCLUSION

For centuries the Middle-East has been ill-served by foreign intervention, both military and political. The focus of the Western nations on this part of the world increased considerably after the discovery of vast oil reserves in the region. However, it is manifestly clear that the interventions were all, without exception, self-serving and that none of the intervening powers had more than a passing understanding of the unique cultural, social and religious norms of the region. They were almost unaware of the central role of tribal loyalties and the strict paternalistic foundation of the society. This anomaly continues to this day. There does not seem to be any possibility of the on-going military intervention coming to a 'graceful' end any time in the future. In this respect, 2015 can be considered one of the worst years in the turmoil that has engulfed the Middle-East, particularly Iraq and Syria, for the past decade and more.

The Middle-East is the home of almost all violent Islamic jihadist movements, irrespective of the cause that created a particular movement or the intensity of their operations. All these movements feed off the now-entrenched religious fundamentalism and without any doubt, Saudi Arabia can be delineated as the one single nation that has contributed the maximum to the current complex situation. The Saudi Arabian monarchy has supported a particularly virulent and fundamental strain of Islam and propagated it outside the kingdom with open financial support for the propagation of the Salafist Wahabi strain of Islam. The idea was to keep the fallout of fundamentalism away from the kingdom, forgetting that such a situation is impossible in today's interconnected world. Saudi Arabia may yet have to reap the whirlwind that it has sown over the past decades.

The United States, the prime mover of all the actions that have been initiated in the region for the past few decades, has been meddling in the Middle-East for a long time but without any visible long-term policy other than unequivocal support for Israel and Saudi Arabia. In the current Syrian

Civil War and the fight against the IS, the US strategy remains rudderless. The most powerful nation on earth is acting as the cheerleader for Saudi Arabia, in their pitiful intervention in Yemen and is seen at its indecisive best in the anti-IS conflict. In 2015, it was seen that the great oratorical rhetoric of President Obama was incapable of carrying the day. Rhetoric can never replace reasoned strategy that is forcefully enforced.

The US suffers from trying to see all events in black and white, as being either good or evil, based completely on their own narrow and partisan perceptions and understanding of what is good and what is bad. Even this slightly skewed way of looking at politics could be accepted, if the US could bring some consistency to the application of their sanctimonious sense of right and wrong. Unfortunately the proclivity of the nation to be selective in the application of high-sounding principles and the rapid changes of opinions instituted to suit themselves has resulted in a heavy loss of global prestige for the nation. Its allies now weigh the pros and cons of their alignment more carefully than ever before.

In 2015, the US continued to display a studied and congenital blindness towards the duplicity of Pakistan in dealing with the US and its own neighbours. The billions of dollars that was pumped into Pakistan to fight the Taliban and al Qaeda was diverted by the country for its own purposes and to support its national agenda, a fact that was reported by a US audit. However, the dichotomy did not register in Washington. In the Middle-East the US continued to support the Kurds since they were the only forces on the ground who were actually fighting the IS, while all the other so-called anti-IS groups gladly accepted arms and equipment from the Western governments only to meekly hand them over to the IS. However, true to form the US was quick to look the other way when the Turks started to bomb the Kurds and their military facilities after Turkey reluctantly entered the conflict. The US is looking more and more like an untrustworthy and recalcitrant ally.

By the end of 2015 it was clear that the Western nations were in a quandary regarding the way forward in the Middle-East. It was clear that the IS had become a global threat and that the regional partners of the Western coalition needed to be coerced into adhering to international norms in dealing with it. There is a need for a new strategy to confront and defeat the IS, one that goes beyond the use of sophisticated air power alone. The events of 2015 demonstrated that the Middle-East is now ruled by 'small men', people who are incapable of rising above petty partisan politics and who do not have the capacity to create and follow a long-term vision of global security. They are bogged down in religious schisms and sectarian divisions.

The best scenario that can be envisaged for the war-raved region in the coming year is a stop to further deterioration of the situation, since any improvement is currently impossible to conceive. In this particular case, hope does not spring eternal....

www.ingramcontent.com/pod-product-compliance
Lightning Source LLC
Chambersburg PA
CBHW060836100426

42814CB00016B/404/J